THE Hooktionary

A CROCHET DICTIONARY OF 150 MODERN TAPESTRY CROCHET MOTIFS

BRENDA K.B. ANDERSON

DAVID & CHARLES

www.davidandcharles.com

Contents

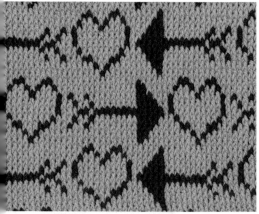

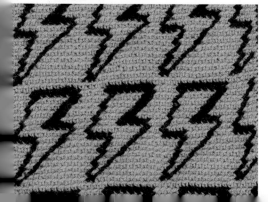

Introduction

There are so few books about crochet colorwork—especially compared to knitting. This has always surprised me, since it is such a beautiful craft and there are so many different styles and variations! Perhaps it is because there are so many different approaches, and things to consider that making a book specifically for crocheters has become a daunting task. Whatever the reason, I've fallen in love with crochet colorwork and as anyone who has ever been in love knows... I just want to talk about my new love. All. The. Time. And what better audience than fellow crocheters?

It is true that you can use knitting color charts to crochet from—in fact, this book began as a sort-of sister book to Andrea Rangel's *Alterknit Stitch Dictionary* book. Her knitting stitch dictionary was inspirational to me, and it made me want to create an equivalent just for crocheters. I had tried out many of her knitted swatches in my crochet. But in order to have a successful colorwork project you will need more than just a great chart. You will need to understand crochet stitch anatomy: how the type of stitch that you use affects both the appearance of the colorwork, and the drape of the fabric (this makes a huge difference!) and how to make choices about gauge (tension), floats (or no floats), and yarn type to create a project that you will be proud of. My goal in writing this book is to take the guesswork out of crochet colorwork so that you can be confident when creating something new. I hope that you find inspiration in my stitch motifs, as I did in Andrea's. I absolutely cannot wait to see what you do with them!

Note: Just to avoid confusion, in this book I will be using the term "stitch pattern" to refer to the anatomy of the stitches you make—not to be confused for "colorwork". For example, in this book I often use the extended single crochet "stitch pattern" to work from the charts. I use the term "colorwork" to refer to the charted images in this book (or the pattern of colors used in each motif).

WHAT EXACTLY IS CROCHET COLORWORK?

Crochet colorwork simply put means crocheting with two or more colors. This can be done in many different ways, with so many different resulting types of fabric. In this book, I've chosen to focus on one method as I think it works well for many different types of projects and color patterns, and it is fairly straightforward to design with. Often this type of colorwork is called stranded crochet, or tapestry crochet, but the definitions of each of these terms vary and it can be quite confusing so I've chosen to define the colorwork used in this book below:

This colorwork is worked in the round with the right side always facing or, as in the case of the Tread Scarf (see The Projects), each row is worked from right to left (left to right if left-handed) and then fastened off at the end of each row. The right side is still always facing here even though it is not technically worked in the round. When using this style of colorwork you will always bring the non-working color along as you work: you can crochet over it, encasing it with your stitches, or you can carry it along behind your work, leaving floats along the wrong side of your work.

How To Use This Book

In this book there are 150 colorwork stitch patterns—each one worked up into a crocheted sample. I chose one specific stitch pattern to go with each colorwork chart, but feel free to swap out one stitch pattern for another. The five stitch patterns I've used are comparable in size and shape, and with a little know-how (as provided in the Comparing and Choosing Stitch Patterns section), you can make an educated guess (before you begin to swatch) as to the look and feel of using another stitch pattern instead of the one pictured. There are also five projects featuring colorwork included at the end. These projects are all classic designs to be used over and over, each time creating something new by switching out the charts for something else. Use the section Swapping and Modifying Charts to help you customize your project with a new chart.

THE SWATCHES

Because the swatches in this book are not pictured to scale, I thought it would be helpful to list the gauge (tension) for each stitch type. Gauge varies greatly from person to person, (and would be much different in another yarn weight) but just for a jumping off point here are the gauges of the five different stitch patterns used in the swatches in this book. All were made with the same DK weight yarn (Berroco Ultra Alpaca Light) and a size F/5 (3.75mm) hook and crocheted over the non-working yarn (no floats) EXCEPT for the swatches that were made in FPDC—those all have floats. All swatches have been steam-blocked, and the swatches that tend to "drift" to the side have been straightened out in the blocking process (See Comparing and Choosing Stitch Patterns for more info).

Extended Single Crochet (ESC): 16 sts and 14 rounds = 4 x 4in (10 x 10cm).

Split Extended Single Crochet (SESC): 16 sts and 20 rounds = 4 x 4in (10 x 10cm).

Center Single Crochet (CSC): 18 sts and 23 rounds = 4 x 4in (10 x 10cm).

Single Crochet through the Back Loop Only (SCBLO): 18 sts and 16 rounds = 4 x 4in (10 x 10cm).

Front Post Double Crochet (FPDC): 19.5 sts and 16 rounds = 4 x 4in (10 x 10cm).

Note: I chose the Berroco yarn because I wanted to use a yarn that was soft, had great drape, had enough stitch definition so that the colorwork was clear, but I also wanted it to be fuzzy enough (have enough halo) so that the stitches would create a cohesive image. I wanted to make sure it wasn't splitty, or sheddy and that it came in a bazillion colors. Basically, I wanted to choose a yarn that would really show off crochet colorwork AND be easy to use. And it had to be something that could be made into mittens, a hat, a sweater, or blanket, etc. This yarn was all of these things. Love. Love. Love!

DECISIONS, DECISIONS!

Before you begin crocheting from a color chart, you have many things to consider—and they are all interconnected. The type of yarn, gauge/hook size, and stitch pattern will all affect the drape of your fabric. The same choices will also affect the appearance of the colorwork (how well the color pattern reads). So regardless of where you jump into the decision-making process, you will need to answer many questions to get the combination of all of these different aspects to deliver the desired end result (a project that makes you want to jump up and down with a big smile on your face!). As always, making a swatch is the best way to learn how a particular yarn-gauge-stitch-pattern-combination will look. However, as someone who generally prefers to throw caution to the wind and skip the swatch, I wanted to walk you through my decision-making process so that you will be able to make a more informed decisions from the start. I'm not saying that you should skip the swatch—please don't—it really is the best way to learn! But whether you are a swatcher or not, if you read through this book, you will be able to make better informed decisions. And P.S. I'm not really a swatcher—but guess what? I made over 150 swatches for this book... so I know even reluctant swatchers can do it!

ABBREVIATIONS

Here's a list of the abbreviations used in this book:

beg:	beginning
BLO:	back loop only
CC:	contrast color
ch:	chain(s)
ch-sp:	chain space
cont:	continu(e)ing
CSC:	center single crochet
CSC2tog:	center single crochet 2 stitches together
dc:	double crochet
dec:	decreas(e)ing
ESC:	extended single crochet
ESC2tog:	extended single crochet 2 stitches together
foll:	follow(s)ing
FPDC:	Front Post Double Crochet
hdc:	half double crochet
MC:	main color
ModESC2tog:	modified extended single crochet 2 stitches together
PM:	place marker
rem:	remain(ing)
rep:	repeat
RS:	right side
sc:	single crochet
sc2tog:	single crochet 2 stitches together
SCBLO:	single crochet through back loop only
SESC:	split extended single crochet
sl st:	slip stitch
sp:	space
st(s):	stitch(es)
WBS:	Work Beginning Steek
WES:	Work Ending Steek
WS:	wrong side
yo:	yarn over

FOLLOWING THE PATTERNS

The patterns in this book use US terminology. If you are used to following UK terms, here's a handy conversion table:

US TERM	UK TERM
Single crochet	Double crochet
Half double crochet	Half treble crochet
Double crochet	Treble crochet
Treble crochet	Double treble crochet

A GENTLE NOTE ABOUT BLOCKING (HEY NON-BLOCKERS—PLEASE READ THIS!)

OK, so I've already admitted that I'm really not much of a swatcher... but I have more to confess. Up until I made this book, I was not really a blocker either. (You: Gasp!) In fact, I really only blocked my projects if they looked uneven. Even out of the 100s of projects I had made for magazines, many of those were not blocked because I didn't think they needed to be. Why am I telling you this, you might ask? Even though I hardly ever blocked anything, I did block every single thing in this book. The reason is: this type of stitching really benefits from blocking. The colorwork patterns look so much more even, the stitches line up better, and blocking helps to even out the look of your fabric as you transition from working in colorwork to working with just one color. And as an added bonus, blocking adds drape to the fabric. Please don't skip this step—it makes a huge difference!

For wool, or other animal fibers: Wet blocking gives you the most control. To wet-block your project, soak it in a tub of room temperature water until it is fully saturated. Remove the project from the water and gently squeeze out the excess—but do not twist or wring it. Lay the piece out on a towel or two, then roll up the towels and pat to remove as much moisture as you can. Unroll the piece, place on another dry towel and pat it into the desired shape, using pins if necessary. If you don't have time to wait for your piece to dry completely, you can use a spray bottle to get your project wet enough to shape. This will dry faster than if it has been soaked. But if you have to wear it RIGHT NOW, try steam blocking it instead (see below).

For acrylic fibers: Wet blocking is not as effective on acrylic yarns. For these synthetic fibers I recommend steam blocking. You can use a regular iron, set on high heat with the most steam. Then steam your piece from about 2in (5cm) away (Do not ever touch the fabric with the iron—and be careful not to steam yourself!). It is best to try this on a swatch first so you know how the yarn will behave.

All of the 150 swatches in this book were steam blocked. All of the projects were wet-blocked. And you know what? I am officially a convert—I block nearly everything now.

Choosing Yarn

WEIGHT

To determine the weight of yarn to use, think about the scale of your project. If you are planning to use a fairly large colorwork chart (lots of pixels), you will need to use a thin enough yarn so that the colorwork doesn't get too big. For example, if you are making a pair of mittens with a larger chart, you will need a thinner yarn than if you were working from a smaller chart. Otherwise the chart may not fit on the mittens. Take a look at The Projects section in this book for examples of how the thickness of the yarn affects the size of the colorwork.

FIBER CONTENT/CHARACTERISTICS

To determine the fiber content and the characteristics/construction of your yarn, think about how much drape your project should have, and any other characteristics you would like it to have.

If you are making a basket, tote bag, pillow or other home décor item, drape may not be an issue—in fact you will likely want your project to be stiff and sturdy enough to keep its shape. You may want a little bit of drape if you are making a blanket, but it isn't as important as if you are making a sweater. If you are making something that will be worn you need to consider how the yarn fiber and stitch pattern will affect the drape of your fabric. For example, a cotton yarn with high twist crocheted at a tight gauge (tension) will make a lovely basket or bag because it will create a stiff fabric. However, it will be difficult to make an item of clothing with ample drape in the same cotton yarn. If you want to use a cotton yarn for clothing, choose a finer gauge yarn (possibly one with a loose spin or chainette construction) and work at a looser gauge in order to achieve some drape. (Also see Comparing and Choosing Stitch Patterns to choose one with better drape). If you are making clothing, lighter yarns that have ample drape, such as wool or alpaca, are always a safe bet. Since crochet stitches are generally stiffer than knit stitches, I've found that it can be beneficial to use alpaca yarn (or alpaca blend yarn) to create a fabric with more drape. This was one of the deciding factors when I chose the yarn for the 150 samples in this book.

For cleaner colorwork It also helps to choose a yarn that fills in the spaces between your stitches. High twist, firmer yarns can be a little more challenging to make your stitches look uniform. Avoid splitty yarns if you are using a Split Stitch (also known as a Center Stitch). In this type of stitch pattern, your hook has to go through a tighter space in the center of each stitch, so you can avoid much frustration if you choose a yarn less prone to splitting.

If you are planning to steek your project (see Steeking Without Freaking!), consider using a woolen-spun yarn. This means that the fibers are going every-which way and they are more likely to catch on each other, thus not slip out of place and ravel. Woolen spun yarns are commonly used in colorwork because they are sticky, but also because they are lofty and will fill in the spaces between stitches. Sticky yarns can be more irritating to sensitive skin, however, so think about whether your project will be worn next to the skin (particularly if you have sensitive skin) before you decide to use a woolen spun yarn—although usually these yarns will become softer and more comfortable with wear. Traditionally, people have warned against using alpaca yarns for projects that use steeking because alpaca yarns are more slippery, but I have found that if the steeks are reinforced they will hold up extremely well.

CHOOSING COLORS

Choosing which colors to use for your project is a matter of personal preference as long as you keep one rule in mind: there must be enough contrast between the colors to make the colorwork visible. Contrast happens in two ways: hue and value. Hue is the first way we learn to describe color—think of the colors in the rainbow: red, orange, yellow, green, blue, indigo, violet. Colors that are opposite from each other on the Color Wheel have the most contrast. They are called complementary colors. Colors next to each other on the color wheel have the least amount of contrast. These are called analogous colors. Even though complementary colors have the most contrast, when they are paired with each other sometimes they can confuse your eye. Certain combinations can even create optical illusions—they can seem to vibrate, or create shadows, making your eyes tired. This phenomenon (called "simultaneous contrast") makes it hard to see your colorwork. One way to get around this is to use colors that have different values. "Value" refers to how dark or light a color is. Think about this as mixing paint: If you take a saturated red and mix it with white, you will get a pink. The more white that you add to it, the lighter the tint. If you take the same saturated red and mix black into it you will get a dark red. The more black that you add to it, the darker the shade of red. Combining shades and tints of colors can create strong contrast. Even analogous colors can contrast enough with each other if they are different values.

If you want your colorwork to really pop, you need colors with very high contrast. If you are looking for a more subtle look, choose colors that have medium contrast. For example, in the Fintan swatch, I used a lighter green and a darker green for a more subtle color pattern **(A)**. The colors contrast enough to see the pattern but they don't really jump out at you. In the Claddagh swatch, the yarns didn't have very much contrast. Although they were different hues, they were quite similar in value so the pattern gets lost **(B)**. I re-swatched with a lighter gray yarn to allow for more contrast and a clearer picture **(C)**.

Swatching is the best way to try out your color combinations, but before making a swatch, try these two things:

1. Twist one yarn tightly around the other until you have a twisted strand that measures about 3in (7.5cm) long **(D)**. If you can't discern the two separate colors very well, you may not have enough contrast. Try this with a saturated red and green yarn—it is surprising how muddy it looks! This is a great example of simultaneous contrast.

2. Take a photo of your yarn balls next to each other and then use a filter or app to change it to a black and white photo **(E)**. If you can't tell them apart very well in the photo you may not have enough contrast.

If you don't know where to start when choosing colors, browse through the colorwork projects on Ravelry to see what catches your eye. There are also many websites specifically for choosing colors that look good together—just search "color inspiration website" to get started.

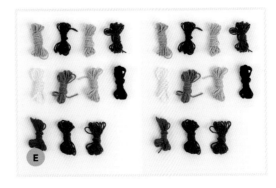

Comparing and Choosing Stitch Patterns

Crocheters can chose from a long list of stitch patterns to use when working in colorwork. Each stitch pattern has its own set of characteristics that affect the appearance of the colorwork, and drape of your fabric. Choosing a stitch pattern can feel like a game of chance unless you have an understanding of how the anatomy of your stitches affects the look of your piece. I've chosen to highlight five stitch patterns in this book because they are my favorites to use for colorwork and they are the most similar to each other in size and shape of each stitch (think of each stitch as being a pixel that has its own specific shape—not a perfect square). Any of the charts in this book can be worked up in any stitch pattern, but it will look a bit different with each choice. This is because each stitch (or pixel) is a different shape—and most of these pixels are not symmetrical from side to side. So when you stack them up together in a grid (as shown in a color chart) they create a unique look.

To help illustrate this, I've worked up the Brick Braid chart and the Peace and Love chart in six different stitch patterns:

1. Single crochet (SC)
2. Single crochet worked through the back loop only (SCBLO)
3. Center single crochet (also known as split single crochet) (CSC)
4. Extended single crochet (ESC)
5. Split extended single crochet (also known as center extended single crochet) (SESC)
6. Front post double crochet (FPDC)

The instructions for making stitch patterns 2–6 are included in the Stitch Instructions. The SC swatches are only included here as a point of reference, as this is such a common stitch.

① SINGLE CROCHET (SC)

This stitch pattern, like many other stitches, drifts off to the right (or to the left if you crochet left-handed). Each time that you take a stitch, you are working it slightly to the right (or left for left-handed crocheters) of the very center of the stitch. As the stitches stack on top of each other you will begin to see that the beginning of the round shifts further and further from your starting point in the first round. As your stitches shift, the colorwork will appear to lean to the side, or twist around your work. If you want your colorwork image to appear vertical, or if you are working a piece that will be steeked (see Steeking without Freaking), or if you are working a rectangular piece (like the Tread Scarf, see The Projects) and you want the ends to be parallel, then single crochet will not work very well. It is because of this that I decided not to include it in the swatch collection in this book. Do not let that discourage you from using single crochet if that is your favorite stitch. If you don't mind the leaning image (it can be quite beautiful), this stitch is still a great choice. Although this stitch pattern is not featured in my collection of swatches, I thought it was important to show a sample here for comparison.

② SINGLE CROCHET THROUGH THE BACK LOOP ONLY (SCBLO)

Working your single crochet stitches under just the back loop reduces the drifting a bit, which also helps improve the quality of lines that slant up to the right (or to the left if you crochet left-handed). Take a look at the Peace and Love samples overleaf, and compare the line quality of the diagonals. The lines that slant up to the right are unbroken in the SCBLO swatch, whereas they appear as a dotted line in the SC swatch. In contrast, the lines that slant up to the left are slightly broken in the SCBLO swatch. The unused front loops in the SCBLO swatch create a strong horizontal effect, and make the right edges of a section of color look a little bit blurred, particularly if it is along an up-to-the-left slanting diagonal. The blurry effect is not particularly noticeable in most colorwork patterns but may be problematic in those with finer details. Working through the back loop only provides maximum drape and makes a very nice, thin fabric.

③ CENTER SINGLE CROCHET (CSC)

Working your single crochet stitches through the center of your stitch causes the stitches to stack neatly on top of one another and also covers the horizontal top loops up completely. This makes your fabric appear very much like knitted stockinette stitch. Because your stitches look like "V"s they are perfectly symmetrical (from side to side) which makes your colorwork look symmetrical too. This is a great stitch pattern for the finer detailed colorwork charts. However, since your stitches are wider than they are tall, your colorwork will appear squat compared with other stitch patterns. In the Peace and Love samples overleaf, notice how elongated the peace signs are in the other stitch patterns compared to the CSC swatch. Because you are working through the center of your stitch instead of the top, you are creating a much denser fabric that has very little stretch. This can be counteracted by crocheting at a looser gauge, and crocheting with floats may help a bit—and/or changing to a yarn that naturally has more drape.

④ EXTENDED SINGLE CROCHET (ESC)

This variation of single crochet increases the height of your stitch, but it also makes your stitch lean a tiny bit to the left (or right if you are left-handed). These leaning stitches actually counteract the drifting in each round that occurs naturally (I am referring to how the beginning of each round drifts a bit with each round worked—see Single Crochet). Because the diagonal stitch shape counteracts the shifting of each stitch, ESC stitches stack up in perfect vertical columns. You will notice that there are slight gaps in diagonal lines that slant to the right (or left if left handed), but that the lines that slant the opposite way are very smooth. This may obscure some finer details, but overall the colorwork will be quite clear. Because this stitch is taller than it is wide, your colorwork might look a bit elongated compared to other stitch patterns. This stitch pattern has wonderful drape, and more stretch than most of the other stitch patterns.

5 SPLIT EXTENDED SINGLE CROCHET (SESC)

Using your hook to split the front legs of your stitch apart so that you can place the extended single crochet between them (instead of in the top, like normal) gives you the advantage of cleaner colorwork for the finely detailed charts. This will make your stitches drift ever-so-slightly to the left (or right if left-handed), however, and it can be a little more time consuming to make this stitch because you need to be so careful about where to insert your hook. Using SESC is worth it if your chart is finely detailed, or if you want a slightly denser fabric than regular ESC, but if you are unsure which stitch to use, I would recommend making a swatch in ESC first before deciding to use the SESC version. It is worth noting that you can work in a combination of both ESC stitches to reap the best of both worlds. For example, in the Mix Tape swatch (see The Swatches), I worked only Rounds 11 and 12 in SESC, the rest of the swatch I worked in ESC. This was because I was unhappy with how the little details in Rounds 11 and 12 looked when I first worked this swatch completely in ESC.

6 FRONT POST DOUBLE CROCHET (FPDC)

Working around the front post of each stitch, naturally keeps your stitches from drifting. This also means that the fabric has vertical ridges that run the length of your piece, and which sit on top of your fabric making it very thick. As you are not working along the top edge of your work, you cannot work over your non-working color. You will need to have strands of the non-working yarn running along the back of your work. These strands are called floats and are common in knitted colorwork (see Sink or Float). Because of the floats, this stitch pattern works best for projects where you will only see one side of the work. The colorwork looks very clean in this stitch— even the finer detailed charts will translate well. Each stitch is equal in length and height, in perfect little square pixels, making it easy to imagine what the colorwork will look like.

Brick Braid is a fine example of a colorwork pattern that makes use of horizontal and vertical lines only. Take a look at the swatches below for a visual comparison.

1 SC

2 SCBLO

3 CSC

4 ESC

5 SESC

6 FPDC

Peace and Love showcases some diagonal lines, as well as some finer colorwork details using round shapes, too.

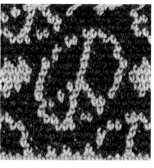

1 SC

2 SCBLO

3 CSC

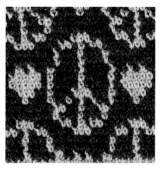

4 ESC

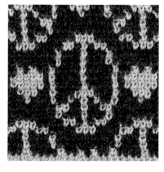

5 SESC

6 FPDC

Why do some stitch patterns have broken lines?

Below is a simplified diagram of how the stitches fit together to illustrate why some diagonal lines appear broken, whereas the opposite diagonal line is smooth. Horizontal and vertical lines are clear in both of these stitch patterns.

SCBLO WORKED BY RIGHT-HANDED STITCHER/
ESC WORKED BY A LEFT-HANDED STITCHER

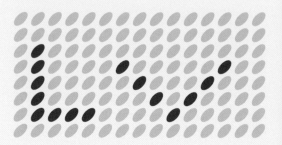

ESC WORKED BY RIGHT-HANDED STITCHER/
SCBLO WORKED BY LEFT-HANDED STITCHER

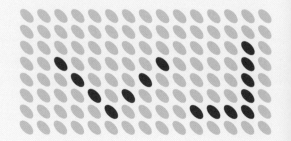

Below is a table summarizing the characteristics of each stitch pattern for easy reference:

Stitch used	Does this stitch pattern drift?	Drape characteristics	Colorwork clarity	Other considerations	Great for these projects
Single Crochet (SC)	Yes—drifts to the right if you crochet right-handed (or to the left if left-handed).	Has medium amount of drape, medium fabric thickness.	Gaps in diagonal lines that slant to the right, also difficult to read finer details.	This stitch can easily be worked at a tight gauge for projects needing a firm, stiff fabric.	Bags, baskets, pillows, tapestry projects using more than two colors.
Single Crochet Through The Back Loop Only (SCBLO)	Drift is minimal—to the right if right-handed (or left if left-handed), can be blocked to get rid of drift.	Has maximum drape, makes a thinner fabric.	Strong horizontal lines may blur the right edge of the image—could make it hard to read finer details, particularly if slanting to the left (or right, if left-handed).	This stitch is difficult to fix later if you make a mistake.	Sweaters, mittens, hats, and other projects that require more drape.
Center Single Crochet (CSC)	Very minimal drift to the left (or to right if left-handed), can easily be blocked vertically (to get rid of drift).	Has much less drape than the other stitches, but remember drape can be improved by using a larger hook or choosing different yarn. Makes a thicker, more dense fabric.	Very clean-looking colorwork as this stitch is symmetrical from side to side. This stitch is shorter than it is wide, so the colorwork image will appear a bit squat compared to other stitch patterns.	Looks the most like knitting, so it is easy to translate a knitting chart into crochet and know what it will look like, and very easy to fix mistakes by making a duplicate stitch on top.	Baskets, bags, slippers, mittens. Projects that benefit from a stiff fabric, or a dense fabric. Also projects that have more fine detail in the colorwork chart.
Extended Single Crochet (ESC)	No drift.	Has maximum drape, makes a thinner fabric with some stretch.	Slight gaps in diagonal lines that slant to the right (or left if left-handed), also may be hard to read some finer details, but overall quite clear.	This stitch is easy to make (not as tricky as the center/split stitches) but colorwork is almost as clear. Easy to fix mistakes. Fabric hangs very nicely (does not tend to curl).	Sweaters, hats, mittens, socks, scarves, blankets, pillows... This is a great go-to stitch for any project that requires some drape. Also excellent for steeking or making a rectangle as there is no lean.
Split Extended Single Crochet (SESC)	Minimal drift to the left (or right if left-handed). Can be blocked nearly straight.	Has medium drape, makes a thin to medium fabric.	Colorwork is very clear. This stitch is taller than it is wide, so the colorwork image will appear to be stretched lengthwise compared to other stitch patterns.	Easy to fix mistakes. Colorwork is as clear as CSC but has a bit more drape.	Sweaters, mittens, slippers, scarves, blankets, pillows. Any project that has finer detailed colorwork.
Front Post Double Crochet (FPDC)	Very minimal lean to the left (or to the right if left-handed). Can easily be blocked straight (no drift).	Has medium drape, makes a very thick and moderately stretchy fabric.	Colorwork is very clear and has excellent bilateral symmetry. Stitches are similar in length and width.	You will need to have floats across the back of your work (no option to encase them). Fabric tends to curl toward the right side at top and bottom edges. Easy to fix mistakes.	Mittens, hats, slippers, pillows. Projects where you want a thick fabric but want some stretch and flexibility as well.

Stitch Instructions

A knowledge of basic crochet stitches is assumed but, for reference, here are brief instructions for standard single crochet and double crochet.

Single crochet: Insert the hook into the stitch or space, yo, pull through the stitch or space, yo, pull through both loops on the hook.

Double crochet: Yo, insert the hook into the stitch, yo, pull through the stitch, yo, pull through two loops on the hook, yo, pull through both loops on the hook.

Here are the step-by-step instructions on how to make each of the five stitches featured in this book. Note: every stitch pattern, except for the FPDC, is shown working over the strand of non-working yarn (encasing it, or "sinking").

SINGLE CROCHET THROUGH THE BACK LOOP ONLY (SCBLO)

Work the first round in a regular SC stitch pattern. On the second round, the SCBLO pattern can begin. The arrow shows where to insert the hook **(A)** under the back loop of the stitch. Insert the hook, yo **(B)** and pull up a loop **(C)**, yo and pull through both loops on the hook **(D)**.

CENTER SINGLE CROCHET (CSC)

Work the first round in regular SC. On the second round, the CSC pattern can begin. The arrow shows where to insert the hook **(E)** between the two front legs of the stitch (right in the center of the "V" that makes up the post of the stitch). Insert the hook, yo **(F)** and pull up a loop **(G)**, yo and pull through both loops on the hook **(H)**.

EXTENDED SINGLE CROCHET (ESC)

Insert the hook (in the usual place, under both loops along the top edge), yo **(I)** and pull up a loop, yo **(J)** and pull through only one loop on the hook, yo **(K)** and pull through both loops on the hook **(L)**.

SPLIT EXTENDED SINGLE CROCHET (SESC)

Work the first round in the ESC stitch pattern (see Extended Single Crochet). On the second round, the SESC pattern can begin. It is exactly the same as the ESC pattern, except the hook is inserted between the legs of the top "V" of the stitch post. The front of the post is made out of two "V"s—one stacked right on top of the other. Align your hook in the center of the top "V" in the post, placement shown by the arrow (but don't push it through yet) **(A)**. On the WS of your work **(B)** there is a horizontal bar just below the top "V" shaped loops (the ones you normally crochet under—not the "V"s that make up the post). You need to push your hook through the center of the stitch making sure that it exits the stitch (on the WS) below that horizontal bar.

Then you make the SESC just like a regular ESC stitch: Insert hook between the two front legs of stitch (right in the center of the top "V" that makes up the post of the stitch), yo and pull up loop, yo **(C)** and pull through only one loop on hook, yo and pull through both loops on hook **(D)**.

FRONT POST DOUBLE CROCHET (FPDC)

Work the first round in a DC stitch pattern. On the second round, the FPDC pattern can begin. Yo, insert the hook from front to back, to front, around the post of the next stitch (from right to left if you are a right-handed crocheter, or from left to right if you are left-handed). The arrow shows where to insert the hook **(E)**. Yo, bring a loop around the back of the post to the front **(F)**, yo and pull through two loops, yo **(G)** and pull through the last two loops **(H)**.

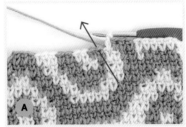

Working From a Color Chart

When working from a chart you will always read it from right to left, beginning at the bottom and working upward as you complete each round. (If you are a left-handed crocheter, please see note below). Each chart square represents one stitch made in the corresponding color. The first stitch in the chart could represent a beginning chain if you are working in joined rounds where the beginning chain counts as a stitch. In this book, all projects are crocheted in rounds without joins, so each square represents a stitch.

Use a post-it note to cover up the chart row above the row you are currently working so you can keep your place. If you use colorwork a lot, consider purchasing a chart keeper: a magnetic board that you can place a paper copy of your chart on, and then use more magnets to cover up the line above to help you keep your place. This may seem like an extra expense... but if you can avoid making just one mistake in colorwork, you'll be glad you bought it.

NOTE TO LEFT-HANDED CROCHETERS:

You naturally crochet from left-to-right, so your crocheted pieces will be a mirror-image of what a right-handed person would make. Most crochet stitches are not symmetrical from side to side. This may be a problem if you work the chart from left-to-right, because of how the stitches fit next to each other. Because of this, left-handed crocheters should make a reverse-image copy of the chart or read the chart while looking in a mirror. In other words, flip the chart horizontally, and work the chart from left-to-right making the crochet piece as a reversed image of what a right-handed person would make. This technique will work for most designs, but for images that cannot be reversed, such as letters or numbers, you need to choose a stitch pattern with more bilateral symmetry, such as FPDC or CSC. This will become clearer when you read Comparing and Choosing Stitch Patterns. The main thing is that you have a choice: either flip the chart image horizontally and work the chart from left-to-right to make an exact mirror image, OR leave the chart as is and work from left to right, which may give a slightly different look, particularly on any diagonal lines or fine details.

HOW TO CROCHET WITH TWO COLORS

Before you begin working with two colors, you must choose whether to crochet over the non-working yarn (encasing it in your stitches) **(A, B)** or to strand the yarn along the back of the work leaving long floats on the wrong side **(C, D)**. Each style can affect the way your fabric looks and feels. You decide: sink or float?

Note: if you are working in FPDC, you cannot work over your stitches as you are not crocheting along the top edge of your work (you are working around the posts at the front). This means you have no choice but to work with floats across the back.

WORKING OVER A NON-WORKING YARN (SINKING)

If you choose to work over and encase your non-working yarn, you will have a fabric that is more reversible **(A, B)**. This is especially nice if you are making a scarf or blanket where you will end up seeing both sides. You also will not need to worry about snagging a finger in a float when putting on a pair of mittens, as there won't be any floats. It's an easy way to manage your yarn as you work—you will not need to remember to twist the yarns together to catch your floats. This is especially helpful if you are using more than two colors at once. Even though this book was written for two-color designs, you can easily use more than two colors per round by just crocheting around all of the non-working colors held together. Crocheting over the yarn can add stability and structure to your work, particularly if you are working at a tight gauge. This can be very helpful if you are making a basket, bag, or anything that needs extra structure. Crocheting over your non-working yarn can cause some bleed through, however. This happens when you can see a tiny bit of the non-working color peeking out between your stitches. This can be avoided by crocheting at a tighter gauge or by choosing a fluffier yarn. A small amount of bleed through, however, isn't very noticeable and may be necessary in order to achieve a nice drape.

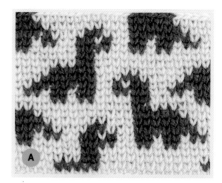

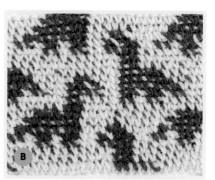

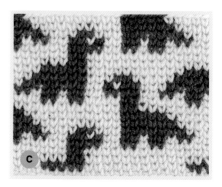

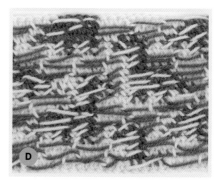

HOW TO WORK OVER THE YARN

When changing color do not fasten off or cut the yarn, but carry the color not in use along the top edge and crochet around it, encasing it with your stitches **(E)**. As you work, make sure that the yarn you are carrying does not constrict your stitches. Every few stitches after a color change, pull on the end of the carried yarn so that you know it is not too loose, then pull on the fabric so that you know it is not too tight. When you need to change colors drop the working yarn and pick up the yarn you have been carrying. **Always work the last yarn over (yo) with the new color on the stitch before a color change.** This is very important—if you do not change to the new yarn at this point your color will bleed into the next stitch, because you are really making the top of the following stitch when you make that last yo-pull-through of the current stitch.

When you are working a round that does not require color changes, you can choose whether to carry and encase the non-working color, or whether to drop it until the next round. Continuing to work over the unused yarn will help maintain gauge and drape. However, remember that your work will only stretch as far as that encased piece of yarn will let it stretch—be extra sure that it does not constrict your work on these rounds. You may choose to drop the non-working yarn to allow your piece more stretch, but this should only be done for a round here or there—not for many rounds as it may make your gauge inconsistent (usually wider).

Always drop the MC to the back, and the CC to the front (or vice versa—just be consistent), to avoid tangling the yarn.

To work joins: On the last yo of the last stitch of the round, use the color that matches the first stitch of the round. Make your slip stitch join with the same color.

If beginning chains do not count as a stitch: Your beginning chain should be in the same color as the first stitch of each round. If the first stitch of the next round is a different color than what is on your hook after the ending join, yo with the new color and pull on the old color yarn tail until the last loop of old color disappears, make your beginning chain, then make your first stitch (in the same stitch as the join).

LEAVING FLOATS ON THE WRONG SIDE (FLOATING)

The main benefit to this is that there will be little (if any) color bleed-through. The other benefit is to allow your fabric a little more drape and a bit more stretch (it will still only stretch as much as the floats stretch). **If your stitch pattern doesn't have more than four stitches in a row of any one color, you do not need to worry about catching your floats.** They will not be long enough to cause a problem, such as snagging on a finger. Otherwise, you will need to do one of two things to catch the non-working yarn in order to avoid long floats across the back of your work:

1. Periodically catch the float in your current stitch about every four stitches or so **(F, top half)**. This means you would place the non-working yarn along the top of the working round and stitch over it encasing it in your stitch, BUT you only do this once every four stitches or so (of the same continuous color).

2. Periodically twist your two yarns (one complete revolution) around each other every four to five stitches or so **(F, bottom half)**. Alternate which direction you twist the yarn each time you do it to avoid a tangling mess.

*Note: the above two methods look nearly identical on back **(F)** and front **(G)**—deciding between them is a matter of preference for the technique used.*

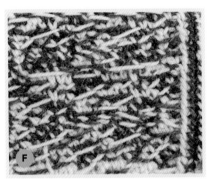

HOW TO WORK COLORWORK WITH FLOATS

When changing color, do not fasten off or cut the yarn—drop the color not in use to the wrong side. If you have more than four stitches in a row, twist the yarns around each other (one full revolution) to catch the float on the wrong side. This can be done after completing one stitch, but before working the next, OR it can be done mid-stitch. For most stitch patterns in this book it works just fine to twist the yarns around each other after one stitch but before the next. When working FPDC stitch patterns it's best to work the twists mid-stitch as follows:

Yo, insert the hook around the post of the stitch, yo and pull up a loop, yo, pull through two loops on the hook, twist yarns around each other, yo **(I)** and pull through both remaining loops. **(J)** shows a float caught mid-FPDC stitch from the wrong side.

Another method is to work over the yarn not in use to catch the float every few stitches—like the sinking method, but in this case you only catch/encase the stitch about every four stitches. Longer floats can get caught on your finger or snagged easily so we want to avoid making them too long.

As you work, make sure that your floats do not constrict your stitches. If you twist yarns to catch a float in one direction, twist the opposite way the next time. This will help avoid tangling your yarn. When you need to change colors drop the working yarn and pick up the yarn you have been carrying along. **Always work the last yo with the new color before a color change.** This is very important—if you do not change to the new yarn at this point, your color will bleed into the next stitch because you are really making the top of the following stitch when you make that last yo-pull through of the current stitch.

On a round that does not require color changes, you do not need to carry the non-working yarn along for that round.

Always drop the MC to the back, and the CC to the front (or vice versa—just be consistent), to avoid tangling the yarn.

To work joins: On the last yo of the last stitch of the round, use the color that matches the first stitch of the round. Make your slip stitch join with the same color.

If beginning chains do not count as a stitch: Your beginning chain should be in the same color as the first stitch of each round. If the first stitch of the next round is a different color than what is on your hook after the ending join, yo with the new color and pull on the old color yarn tail until the last loop of the old color disappears, make your beginning chain, then make your first stitch (into the same stitch as the join).

When working a steek (see Steeking without Freaking!): If you are working in a stitch pattern other than FPDC, consider working over the non-working yarn for the stitches that form the steek. This will reduce the chance of your yarn slipping out of place. This isn't absolutely necessary as the reinforcement stitches will hold stitches in place—it is an additional precaution.

A note about holding your yarn: Because crochet stitches have more complicated motions to them than knitted stitches, it is much more difficult to hold two yarns at the same time as you do in stranded knitting. Crocheting over a strand of non-working yarn adds another layer of difficulty, because it needs to lay across the top edge of your work. This is not to say that it is impossible—I did find videos on the Internet of people holding both strands of yarn at once, but most of us (including myself) will be more successful holding one yarn at a time in their non-working hand. Yes, it does take time to set down the yarn you've finished using and pick up the new color, but you get quicker as you gain experience.

SWATCHING: CHOOSE YOUR APPROACH

To make a swatch of this type of colorwork, you will need to swatch in the round. This can be done in one of two ways: You can double the amount of stitches that you need in 4in (10cm) and make a tube that is 4in (10cm) wide when flattened, or you can make a swatch that can be cut open so that your swatch can lay flat to measure. If you are worried about running out of yarn for your project, you will not want to cut your swatch as it cannot be re-used. However, if you have plenty of yarn I recommend the latter option. If you crochet your swatch with a steek it will be really easy to see where to cut it apart (See Steeking without Freaking!). And, if you crochet your swatch with a steek, you can always unravel it to re-use the yarn **before you cut the steek**.

Steeking Without Freaking!

Steeking is not just for knitters! Wait a second... what exactly is steeking? Let's say you are making a sweater with a colorwork yoke, but you want it to be a cardigan, which buttons up the front. How do you do that when you need to work the yoke in the round? Well you crochet it in the round and then you just cut it up the front for the opening. Say whaaaaat?! Yes, I know this seems crazy, but knitters do it all the time—and so can we!

OK before you freak out, let me say that there are stitches before and after the designated cutting zone that will get reinforced in one of three ways. These reinforced stitches form a seam allowance that will keep your work from unraveling and form a nice protective edge that turns to the inside of your work.

I'll show you how it works on a gauge swatch with a steek. It works for any of the five stitch patterns in this book, and also whether you are crocheting over the non-working strand (I recommend this) or creating floats on the wrong side. However, if you are working with floats, consider working over the non-working yarn for only the stitches that form the steek—this will reduce the chance of your yarn from slipping out of place. It isn't absolutely necessary as the reinforcement stitches will keep your stitches in place, it is just an additional precaution. Since you are not able to work over the non-working yarn when working in the FPDC stitch pattern, just make sure that you reinforce the steek stitches before you cut the steek.

STEEKED SWATCH INSTRUCTIONS

Using main color (MC), ch the number of sts to measure for the swatch + 9 sts (includes 1 st turning ch on Set-up row, 3 steek sts at beg and end of round, 1 ch st on each end to separate steek sts from swatch). For clarity, the steeked sections at the beg and end of the round are MC, then contrast color (CC), then MC.

Set-up row: Beg in 2nd ch from hook and working in bottom of ch, 1 st in next 3 ch, ch 1, skip next ch, 1 st in each st across until 4 sts rem, ch 1, skip next st, 1 st in next 2 sts, 1 st in last ch, adding the CC in last yo of st (in other words, yo with MC and CC held together, and complete last st), cont to hold both strands together, ch 2, drop CC, ch 1 with MC only. Do not turn. Do not join **(A)**.

Round 1: Bring beg of Set-up row around next to last ch st to beg working in the round. Be careful not to twist work. Work over non-working yarn to encase it. Beg with first st of Set-up row, *1 MC st in first st changing to CC on last yo, 1 CC st in next st changing to MC on last yo, 1 MC st in next st (change color on last yo if first st of chart is CC), ch 1 **(B)**, work across, foll chart, to next ch-1 sp (last yo of st before ch-1 sp needs to be MC), ch 1 (with MC), 1 MC st in next st changing to CC on last yo, 1 CC st in next st changing to MC on last yo, 1 MC st in next st making last yo with both yarns held together as one, ch 2 (with yarns held together), drop CC, make 1 MC ch **(C)**.**

Rep from * to ** for each round, ending last round after first ch with yarn held double.

Fasten off **(D)**.

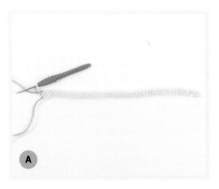

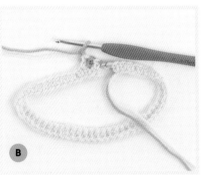

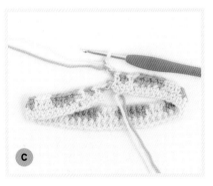

STEEK REINFORCEMENT

Use one of three techniques to reinforce the steek. For best results, reinforce the steek before before cutting it open. However, if you must cut the steek first and reinforce it after it has been cut, that is ok! Just handle it delicately until the reinforcement technique has been done.

METHOD 1: SEWING WITH SEWING MACHINE (OR NEEDLE AND THREAD, BY HAND)

Use a sewing machine to stitch through the columns of steek stitches on either side of the center chain spaces. If you do not have access to a sewing machine, you can sew by hand with a sewing needle and thread, using small enough stitches so that you sew through each crocheted stitch. For best results, use a zig-zag stitch and try to catch two columns at once. For example, in the photo **(E)** you can see that there are two rows of machine stitches on each side of the steek. Each row zig-zags back and forth between the MC and the CC. This makes for a very secure steek.

METHOD 2: SLIP STITCHES (OR SURFACE CROCHET) ALONG THE COLUMNS OF STEEK

Make at least two rows of slip stitches through each steeked section. The dark pink lines were stitched through the CC part of the steek, and the lighter pink through the MC closest to the ch-3 space **(F)**. To do this, place a slip knot on your hook, *insert the hook (from RS to WS) through a stitch at the edge of the steeked section, yo and pull up a loop, continue to pull the loop through the loop on the hook, repeat from * working across the stitches in one column of the steek. Try to insert the hook into the center of each stitch, and not between stitches. This technique works best when the slip stitches are worked fairly tightly, but be careful not to constrict the fabric.

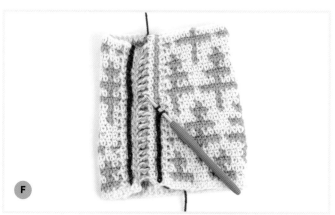

METHOD 3: FELTING PEN

This is without a doubt my favorite method—it is so simple and foolproof, as long as you are working with a wool or other animal fiber that felts. Use a felting pen to lightly felt the steeks so that they cannot unravel. To do this, you simply push the felting pen repeatedly into the steek stitches until they can no longer separate from each other **(G)**. Try to separate the stitches from one another; once felted, this is impossible to do, you are finished. Usually this does not need to look fully felted on the RS.

After reinforcing you are ready to cut straight through the center of the chain stitches **(H)**!

ADDING A BUTTON BAND

To work a button band or edging along the edge of your steek, work your stitches into/under the ch-1 spaces that are right before and right after your steek stitches. This will help the three columns of stitches turn to the WS of your work. Simply turn your work 90 degrees to work single crochet (or another stitch) into those ch-1 spaces **(I)**.

You may need to experiment with different hook sizes, or different numbers of stitches along this edge in order to get the edging to lay flat. If the edge ripples, there are too many stitches in the edging or the hook size is too big. If your edging is making your fabric pucker, you need more stitches or a bigger hook. If one stitch per row constricts the fabric, try two stitches in every-other ch-1 space (and 1 stitch in remaining ch-1 spaces). The Badlands Cardigan is an example of a steeked edge that uses this technique. Although the button band is crocheted separately, it is stitched to a row of SC sts that was worked sideways into those ch-1 spaces along the steek edge. This makes the edge look very polished **(J)**.

A grosgrain ribbon can be hand-stitched (or machine stitched) to the interior edge of steeked garment to hide the steek **(K)**.

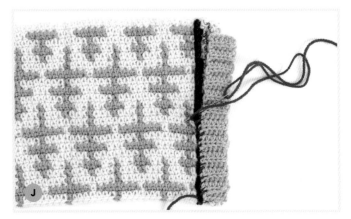

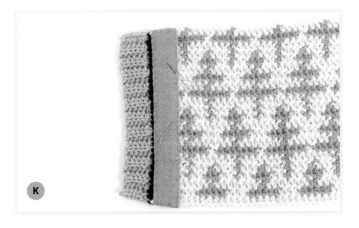

The Swatches

From Bigfoot to op art, this collection includes representational, abstract, and non-objective colorwork designs. The images were inspired by nature, pop-culture, fine art, and a quirky sense of humor.

Molly's Wallpaper

Tip

This is my go-to stitch pattern for colorwork: it's so easy to do and the resulting fabric has such a wonderful drape!

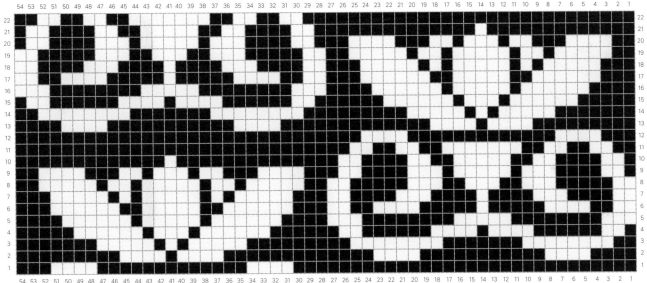

Forest

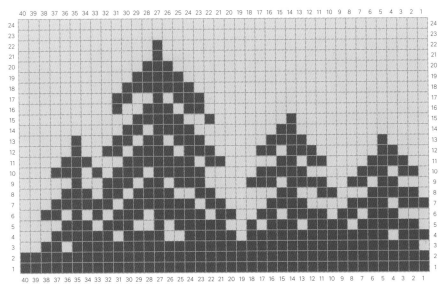

Tattoo

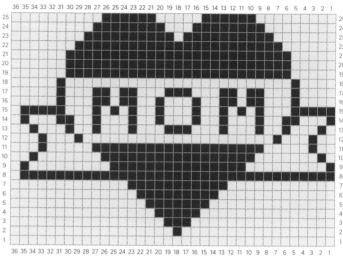

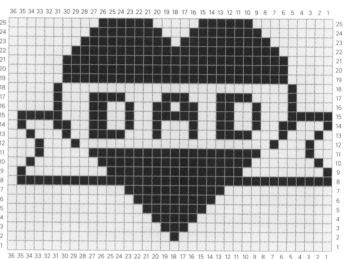

Istanbul

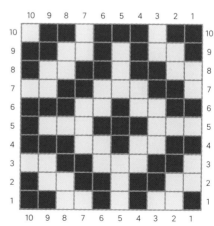

Ramen

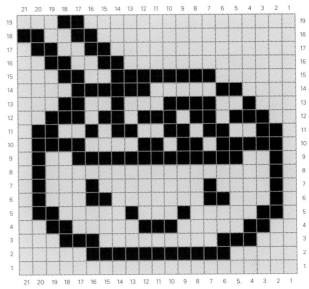

Awareness

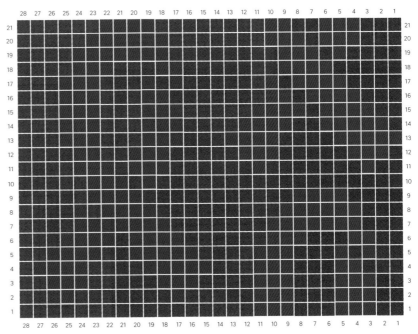

Beaded Curtain

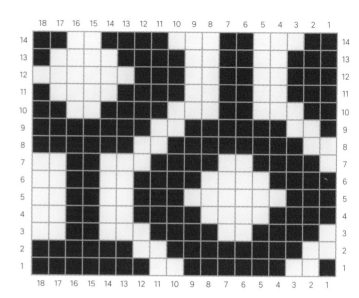

Big Star

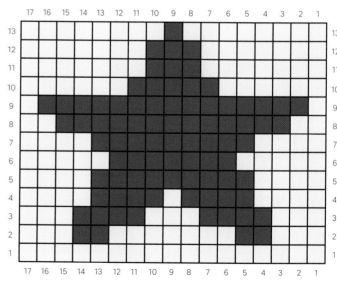

Bison

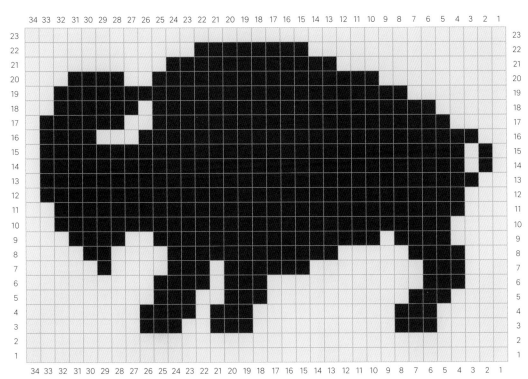

Chained Squares

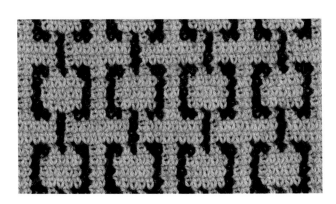

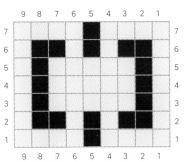

Broken Lines

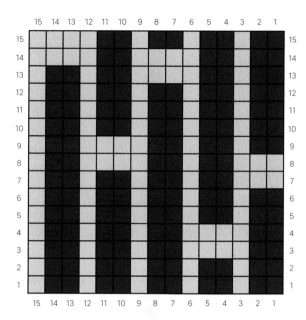

Cable

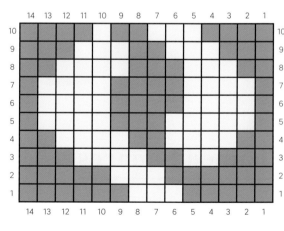

Buffalo Plaid

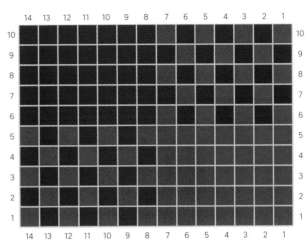

Headphones

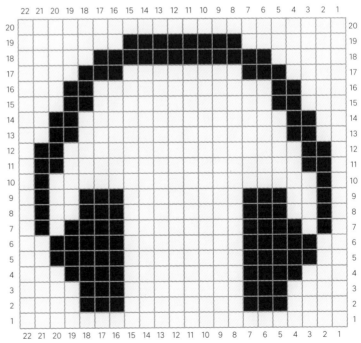

Circles or Squares?

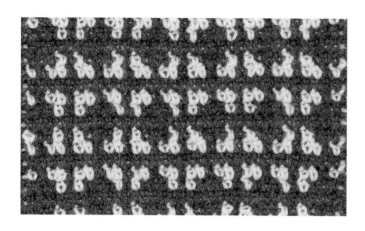

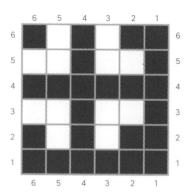

Diamond Mountain

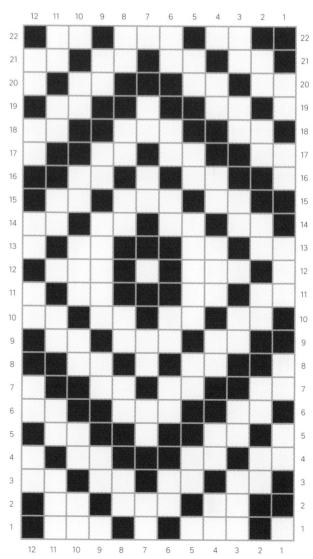

Deco

Tip

If you want to add a little bit of a third color here and there in a colorwork design, using duplicate stitch on a background of ESC (or CSC) is an easy option and looks great. See How To Fix Colorwork Mistakes, Duplicate Stitches for instructions.

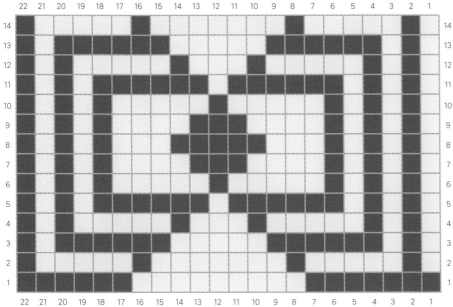

Dogtooth

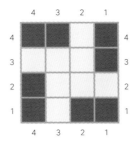

Crisscross Applesauce

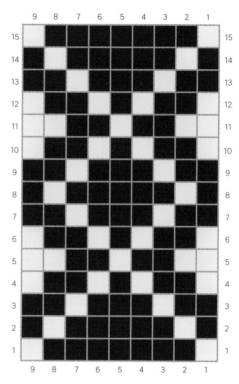

Cupcakes

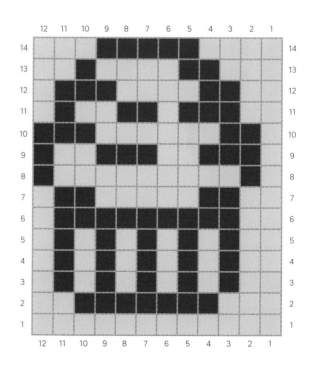

Hot Diggity Dog!

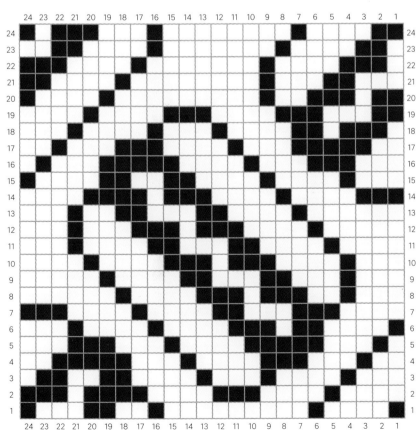

Escher Cubes

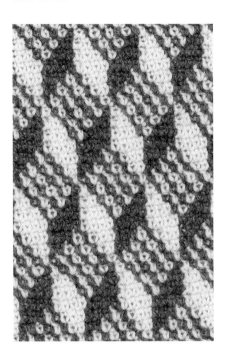

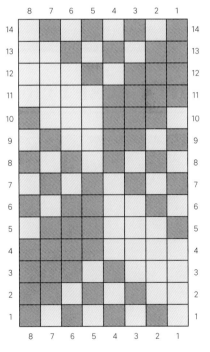

Fintan

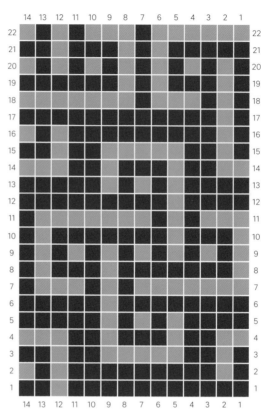

Girl's Best Friend

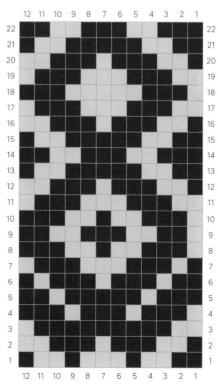

Donuts

| | 38 | 37 | 36 | 35 | 34 | 33 | 32 | 31 | 30 | 29 | 28 | 27 | 26 | 25 | 24 | 23 | 22 | 21 | 20 | 19 | 18 | 17 | 16 | 15 | 14 | 13 | 12 | 11 | 10 | 9 | 8 | 7 | 6 | 5 | 4 | 3 | 2 | 1 | |

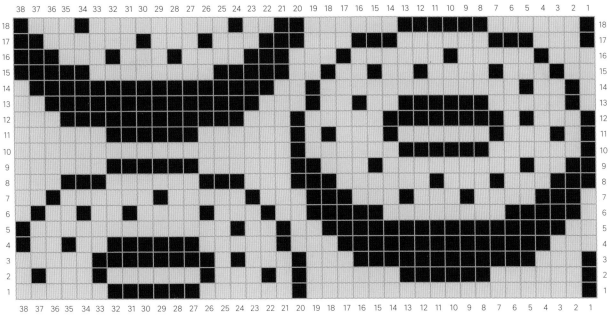

| | 38 | 37 | 36 | 35 | 34 | 33 | 32 | 31 | 30 | 29 | 28 | 27 | 26 | 25 | 24 | 23 | 22 | 21 | 20 | 19 | 18 | 17 | 16 | 15 | 14 | 13 | 12 | 11 | 10 | 9 | 8 | 7 | 6 | 5 | 4 | 3 | 2 | 1 | |

Checkerdot

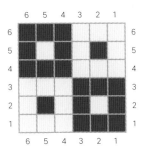

Howl

Vibrations

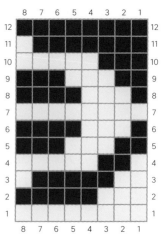

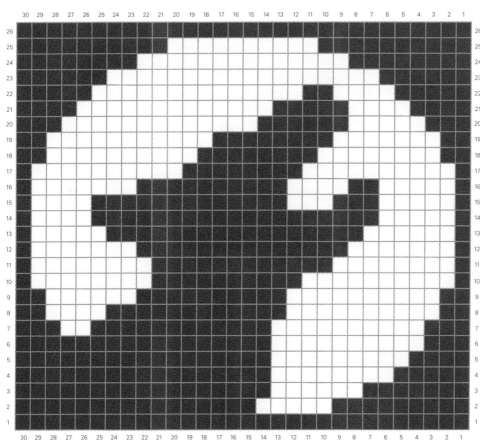

Pinecones

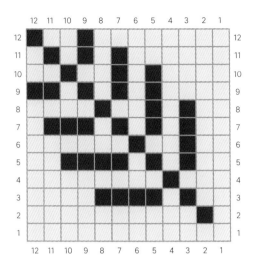

India Palace

Leopard Print

Loop de Loop

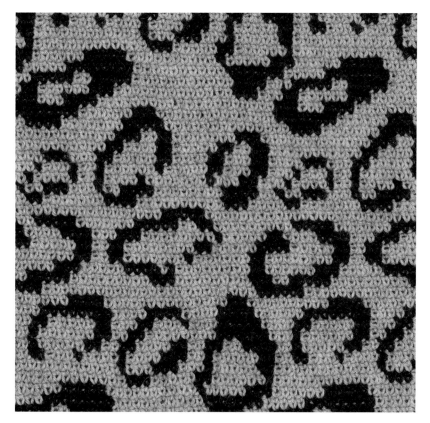

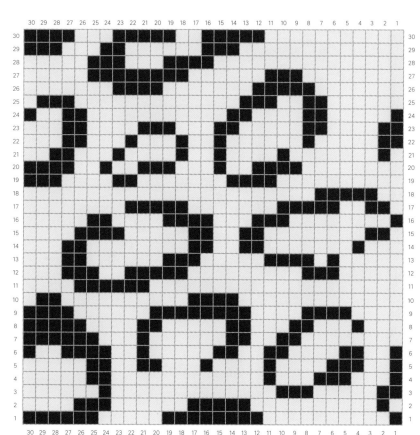

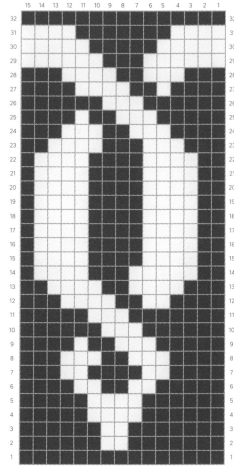

Mix Tape

Open Weave

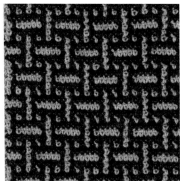

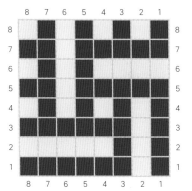

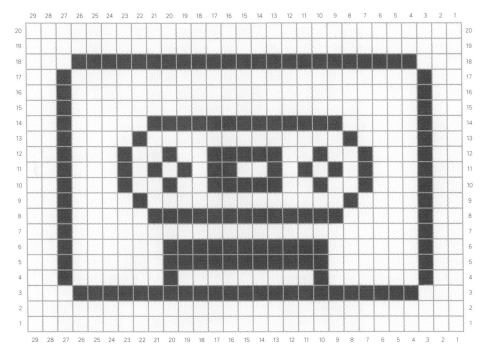

Pint Glass

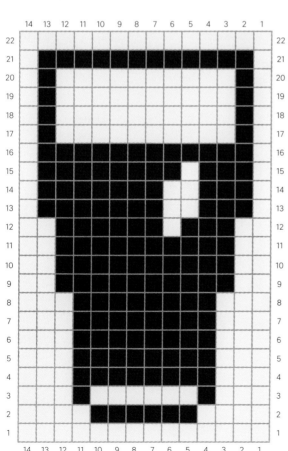

Single Rose

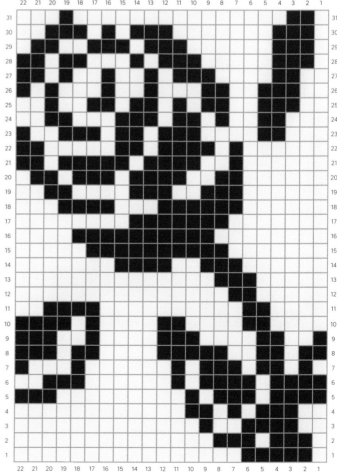

Kitties with Feelings

Tread

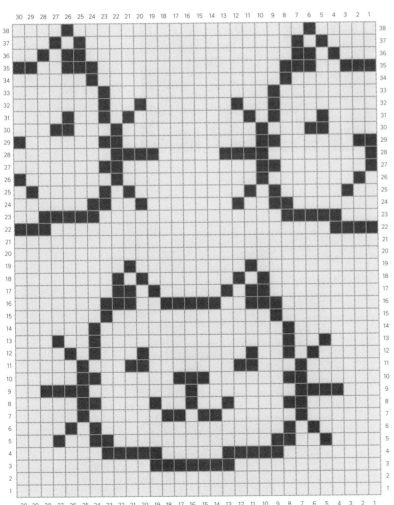

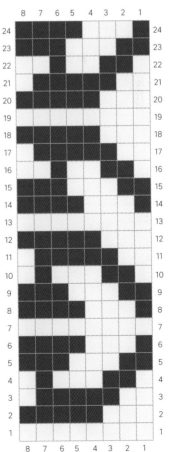

Queen Bee

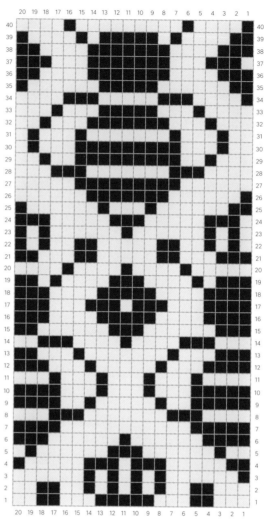

Soft Serve

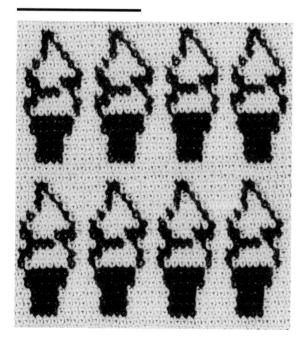

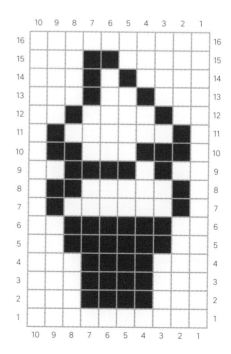

Rainy Day

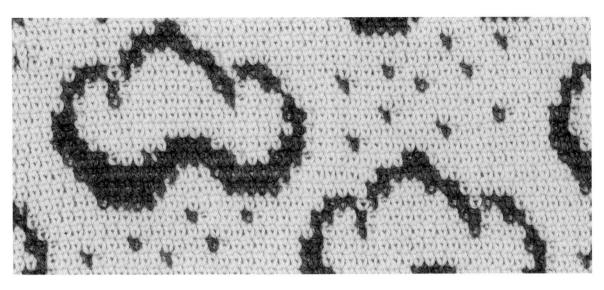

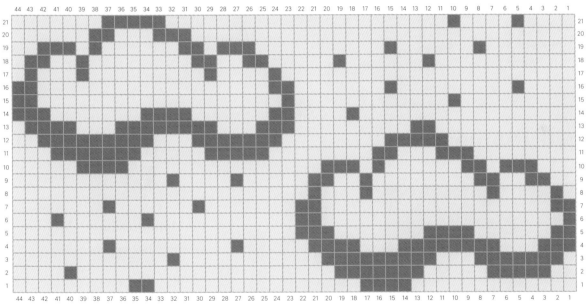

Nautical

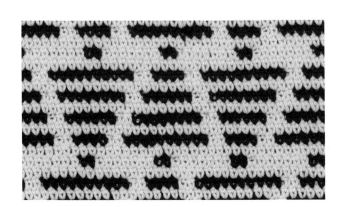

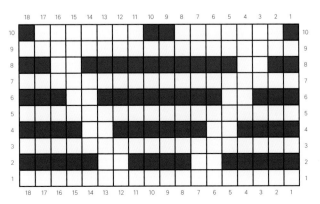

Light as a Feather

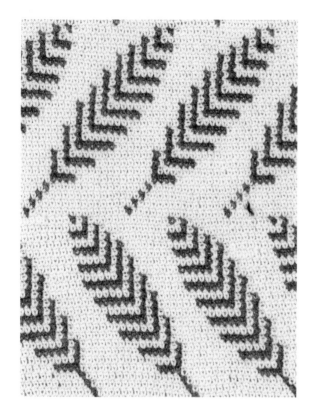

Scattered Diamonds

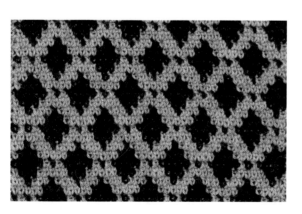

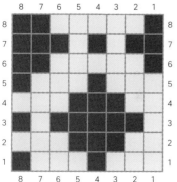

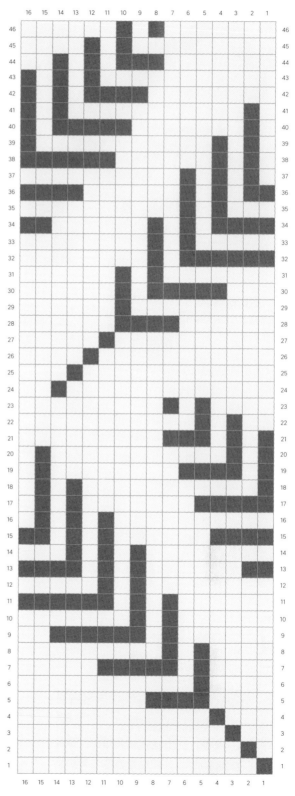

Runs with Scissors

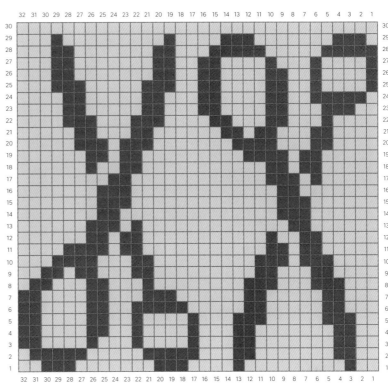

Solano

Spaced Diamonds

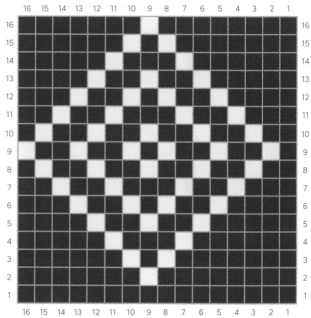

Peking

T.V.

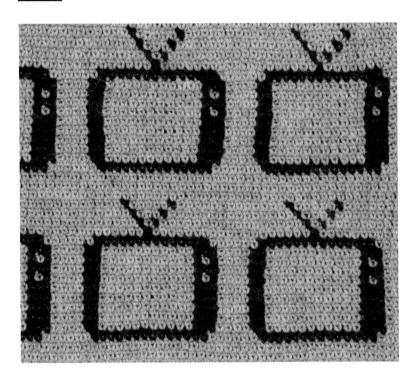

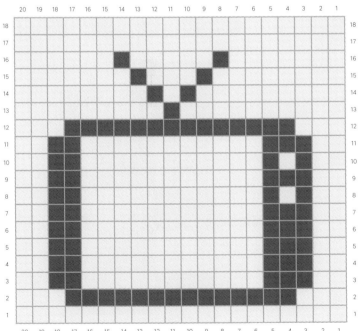

Striped Feathers

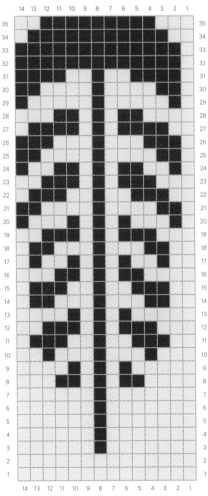

Swallows

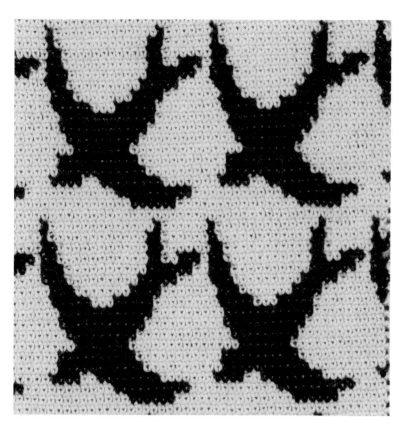

Uneven Floor

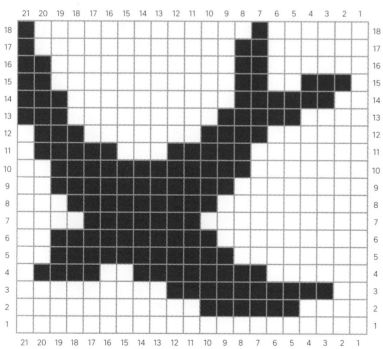

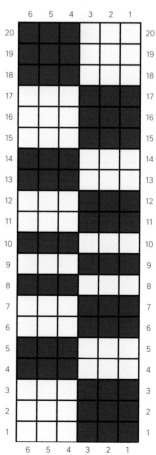

Tesla Coil

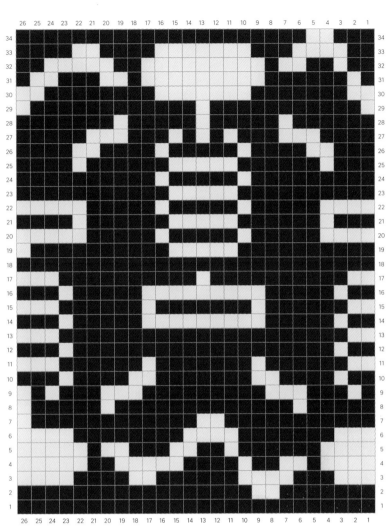

Square Stripes

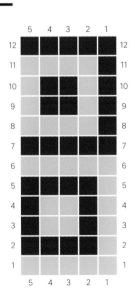

Tip

*The first time I used the ESC stitch pattern
I was designing a sweater with robots
and I needed the robots to have clean,
right angles—this stitch was a perfect fit!*

Icicles

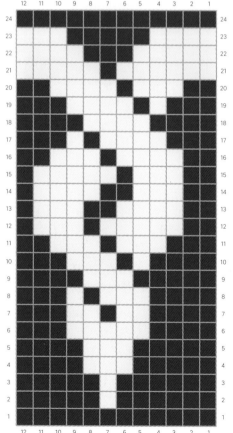

Waves of Grain

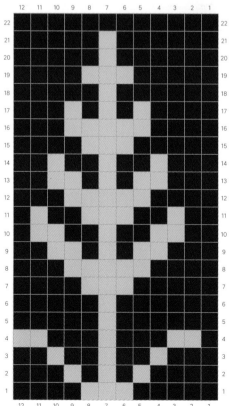

Great Divide

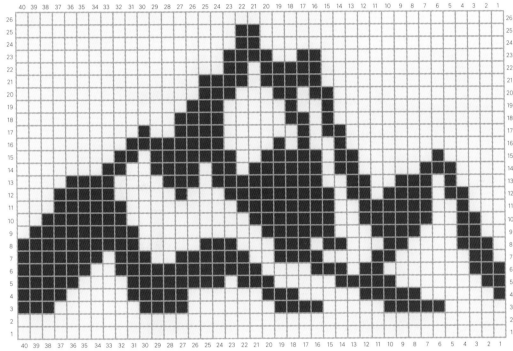

Call Me

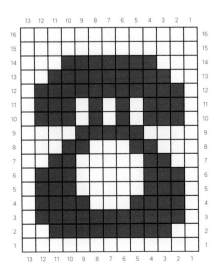

Make a Spectacle

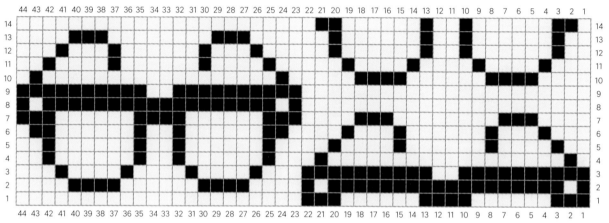

Bonbon

Hidden Circles

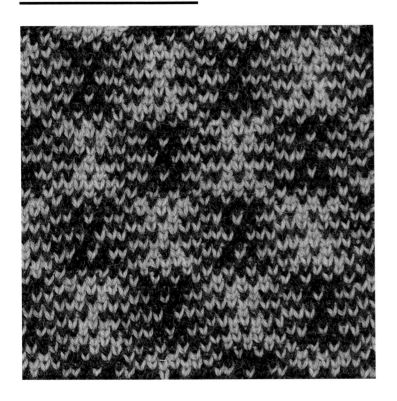

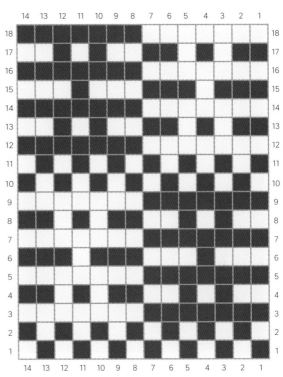

Phases

Carpeted

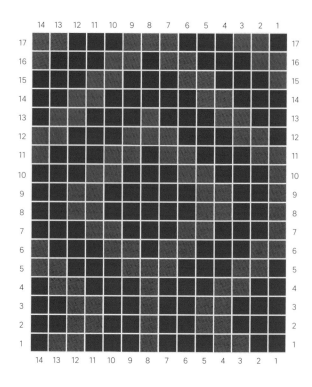

Jackalope

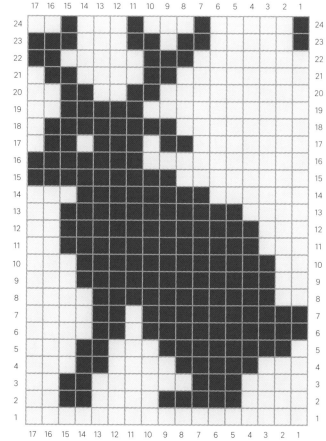

Coffee Cup

Fresh Squeezed

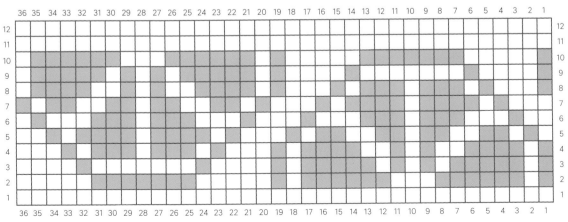

Gardens

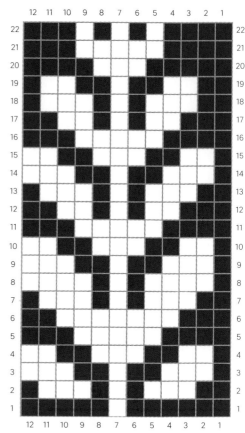

Heart Breaker

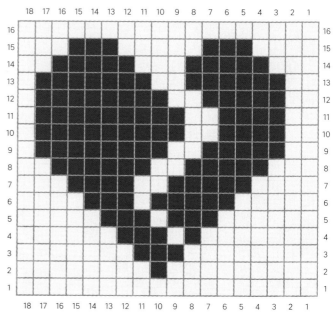

Peaks and Valleys

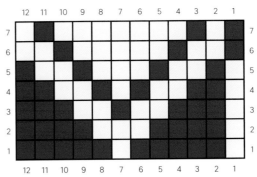

Irregular Zig

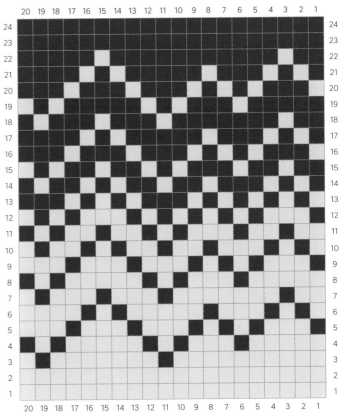

Bosky

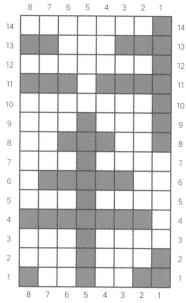

Peace and Love

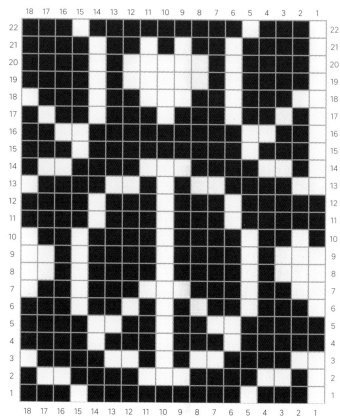

Ceramic

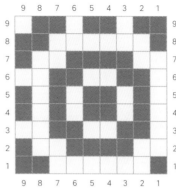

Nessie

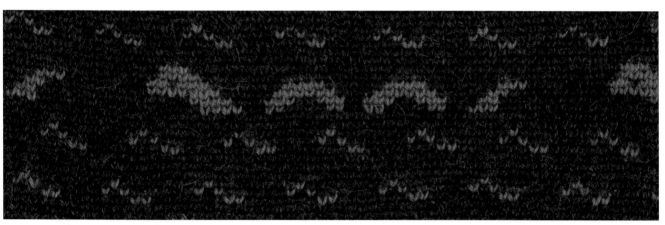

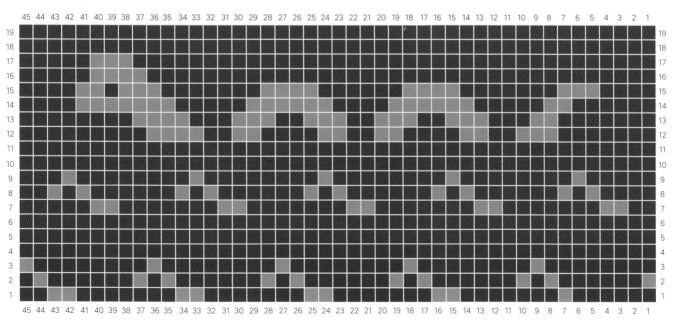

Secret Language of Yarn

Sideways Glances

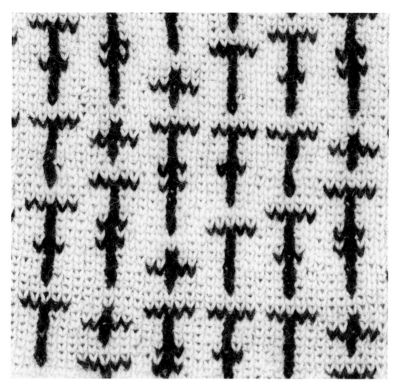

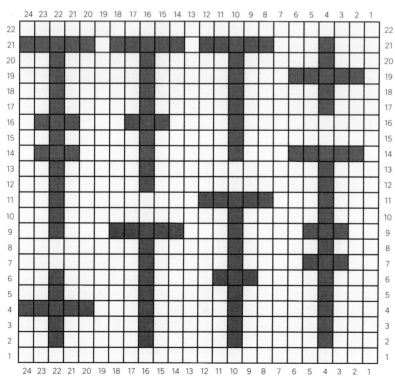

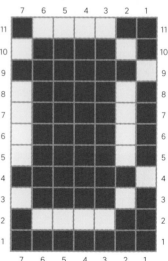

Quilt

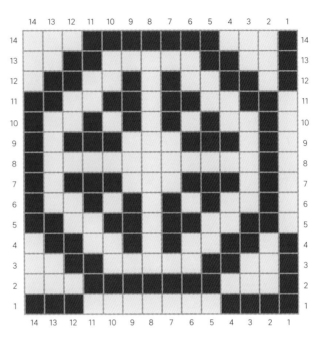

Single Crochet!

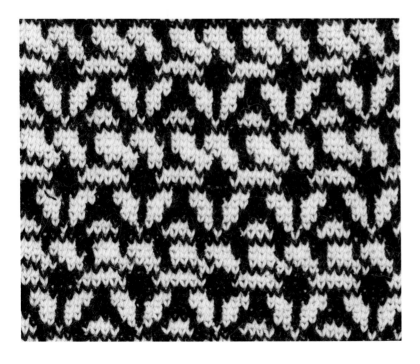

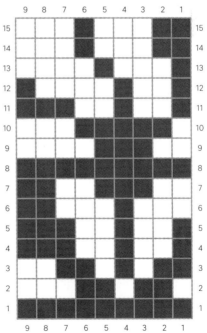

Spatter

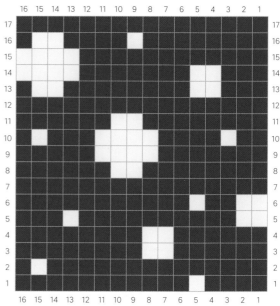

Nellie the Elephant

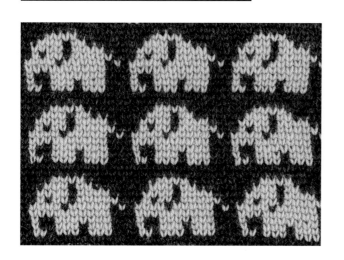
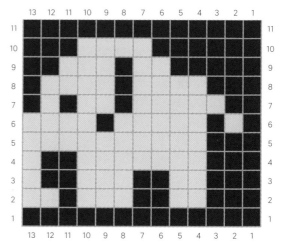

Tiny Dancer

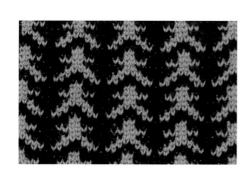
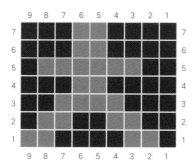

Writing on the Wall

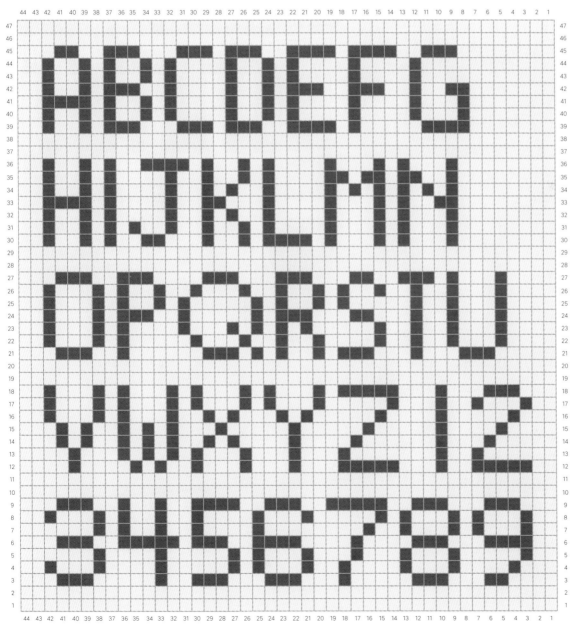

Bubbly

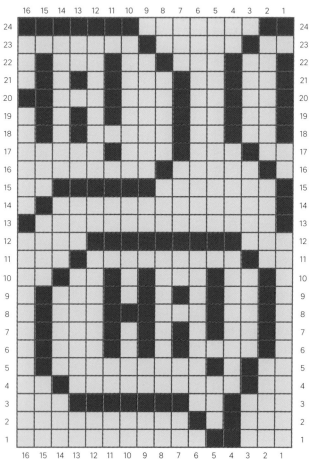

Bunny Love

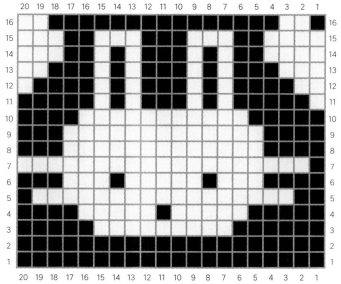

Cherries

Plait

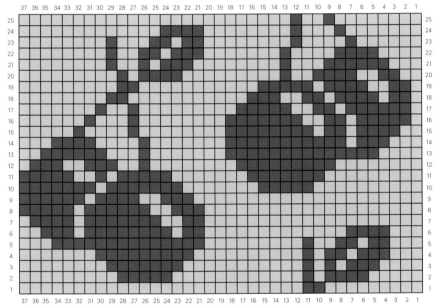

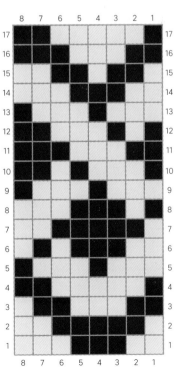

Delftware

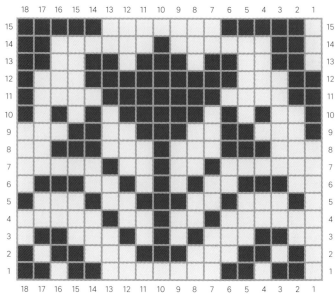

Lucky Horseshoe

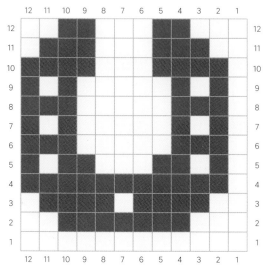

Checks

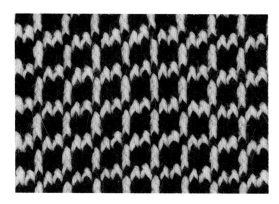

Tip

You may find that the first round or two of the FPDC stitch pattern ends up a little wider than the rest of your swatch or project. If this happens, blocking will help to fix it. Next time try a smaller hook to begin your FPDC piece, or work a bit more tightly on the first two rounds.

Camping

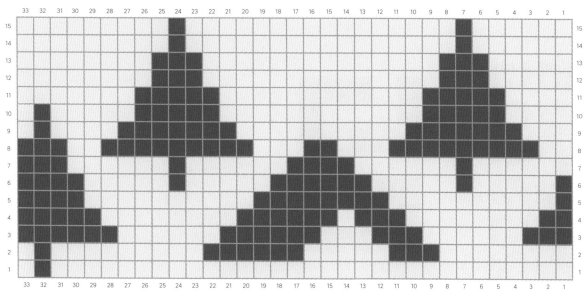

Crush

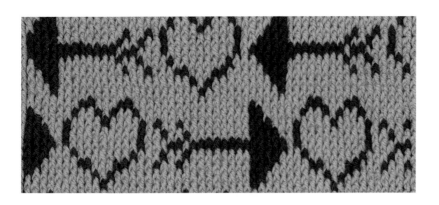

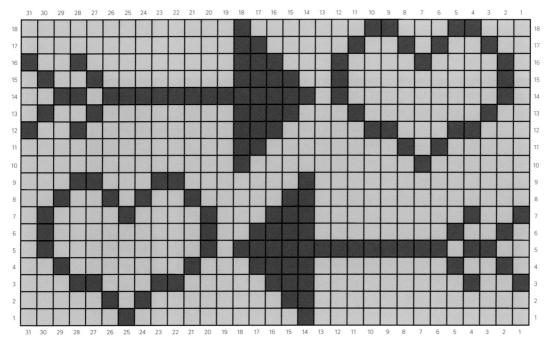

Maps

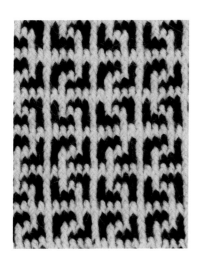

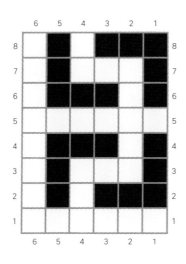

Tip

You can work your set-up round (the round before colorwork begins) in a shorter stitch, like half-double crochet or even single crochet if you want less of it to show. Just remember that you will still need to work around the post when you begin the FPDC colorwork stitches.

Diamondback

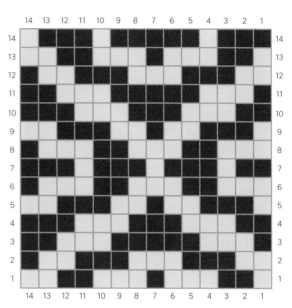

Hand Sign

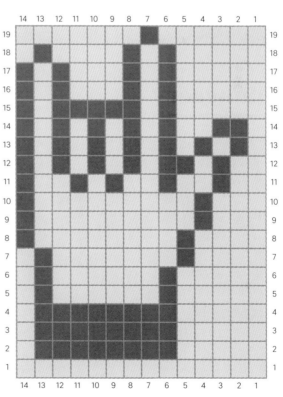

Deciduous

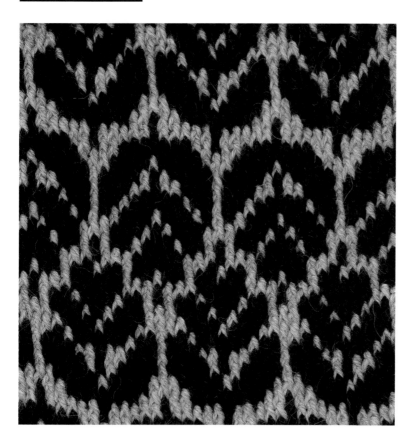

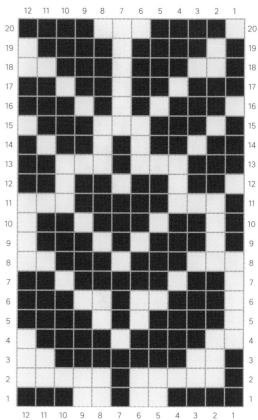

Skulduggery

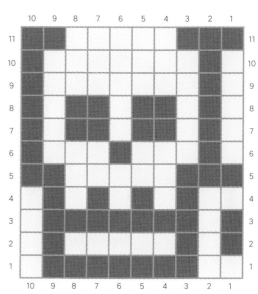

Cross Winds

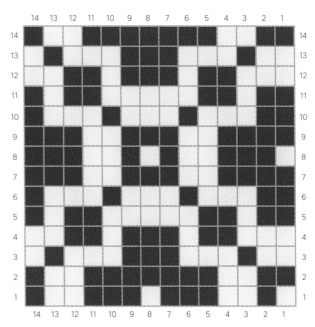

Maki

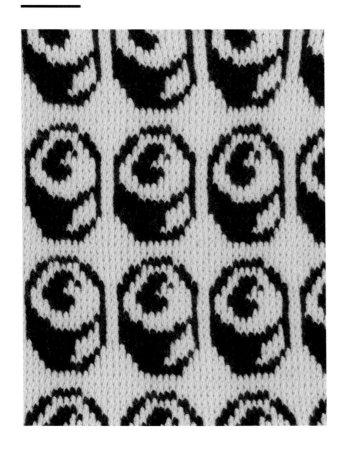

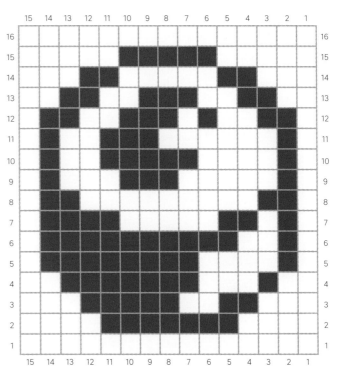

Grout

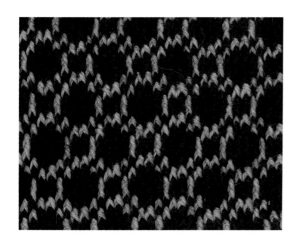

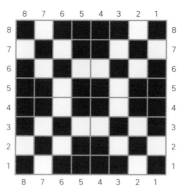

Puppy Love

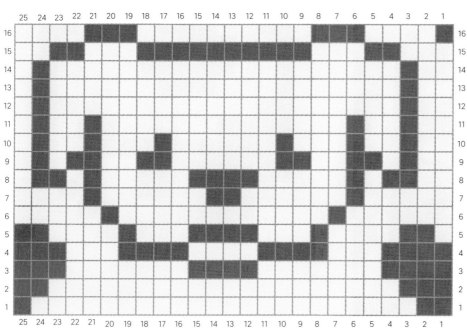

Posy

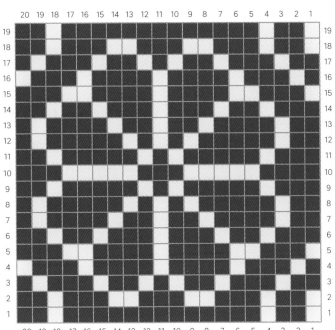

Dinos

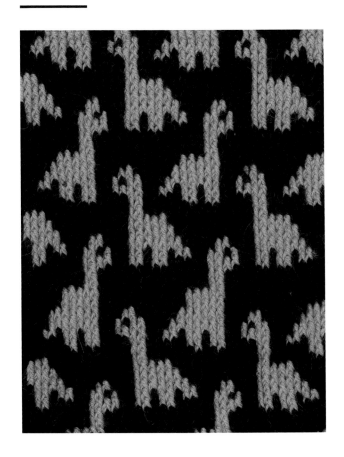

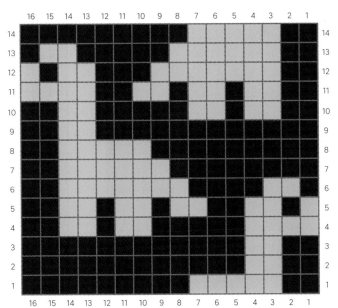

Intersection

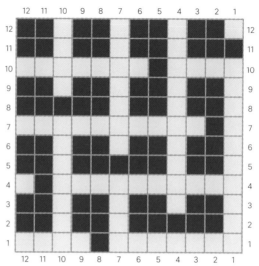

Spiders

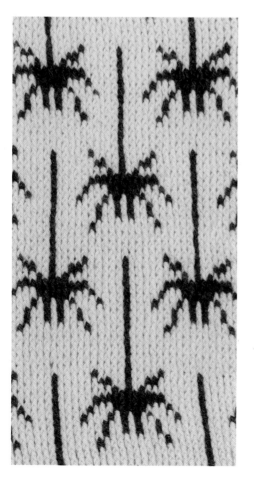

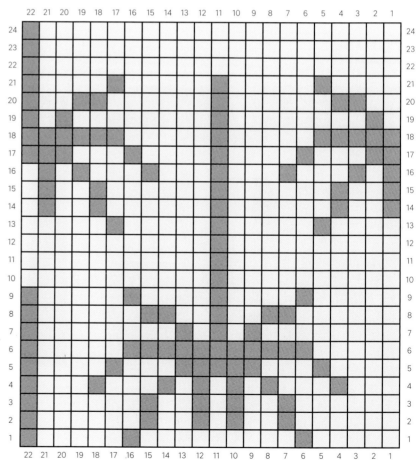

Worlds Collide

Brick Braid

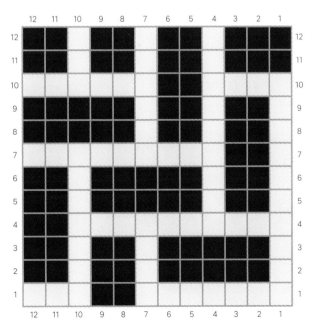

Interlaced Vines

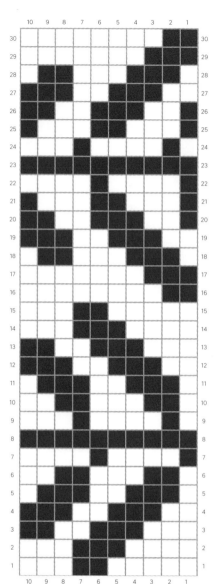

Tiny Unicorn

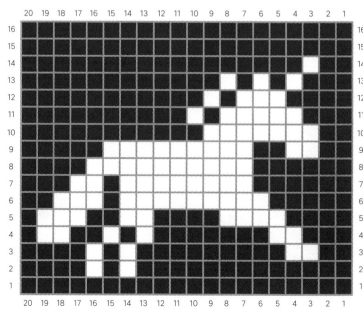

Riptide

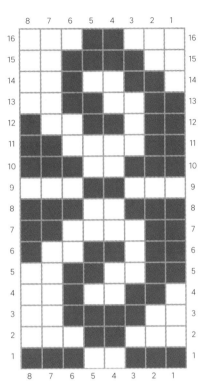

Flip Flop Boxes

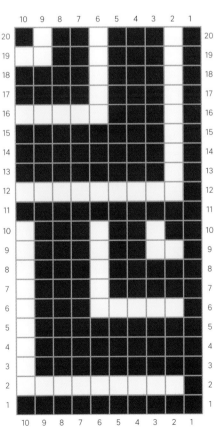

Luau

Bigfoot

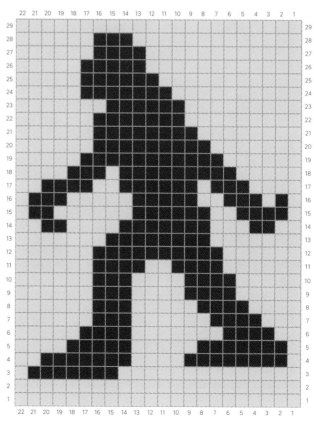

Backbone

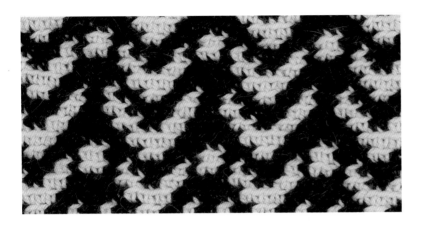

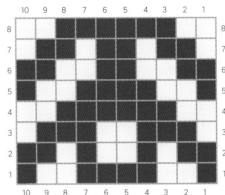

Amplified

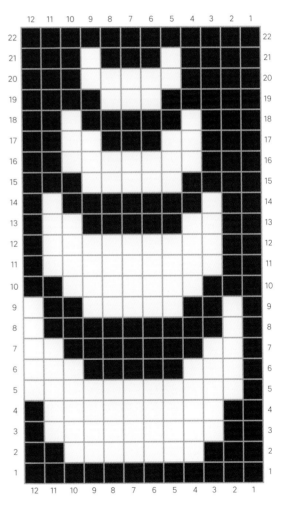

Buckled

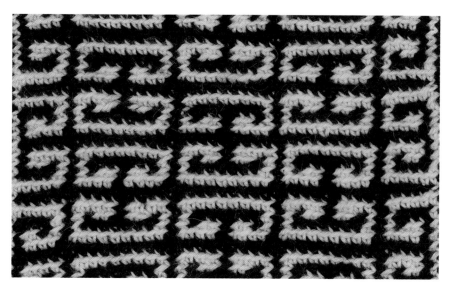

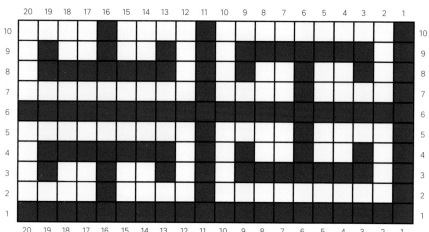

Easter Island

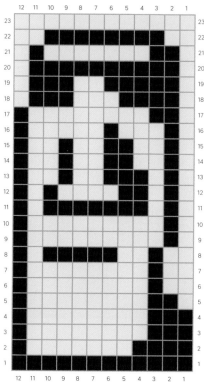

Tip

Try not to pull too hard when you pull up that first loop of the SCBLO stitch pattern—this can stretch out the back loop of the stitch you are working into and cause a hole to form beneath your new stitch.

Bolt from the Blue

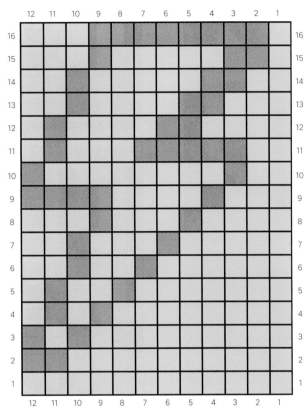

Zigs and Zags

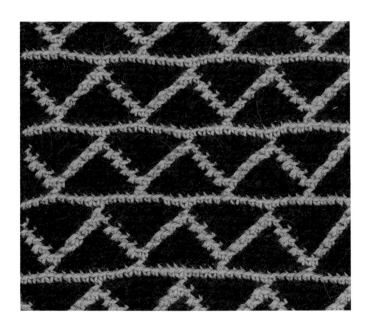

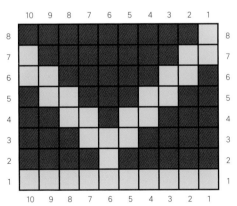

Freeway

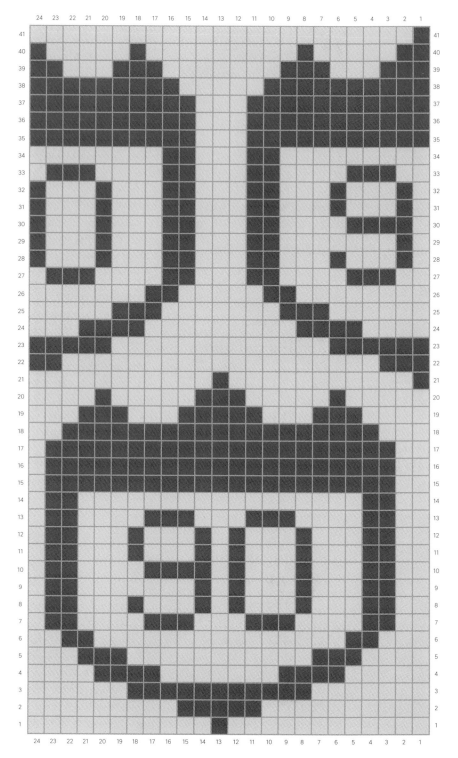

Sliding Tiles

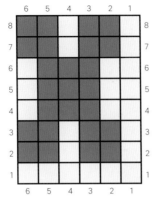

Turn Signal

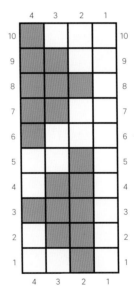

Helix

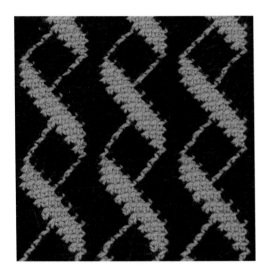

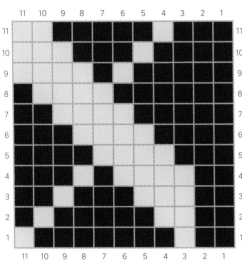

Tip

If you choose a color chart that has strong right-leaning diagonals—for example, "Bolt From the Blue" or "Tooth"—your colorwork will look extra-crisp in the SCBLO stitch pattern.

Setting Sun

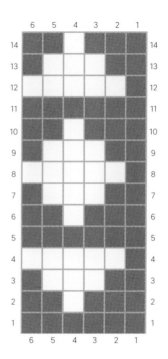

Hearts Together

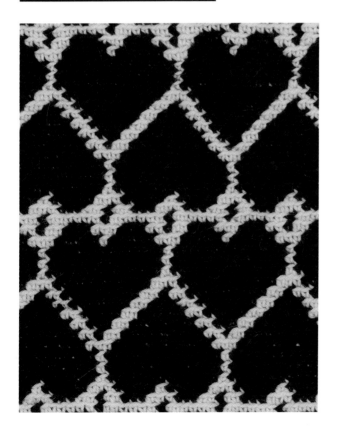

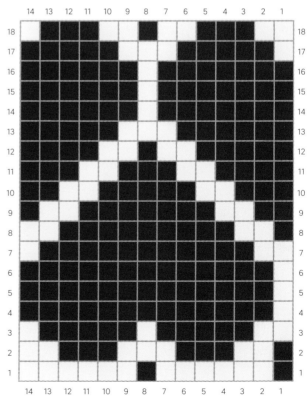

Tooth

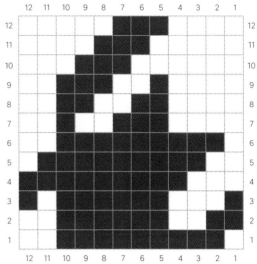

Saguaro

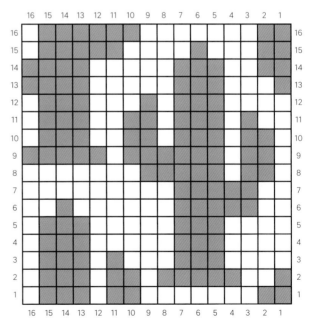

Twin-tone Hearts

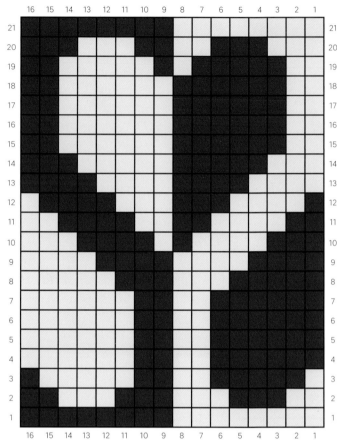

Umbrella

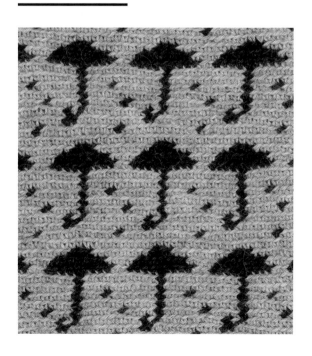

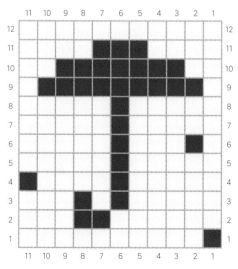

Village

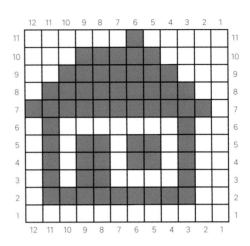

Radiate

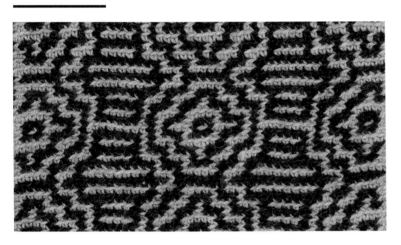

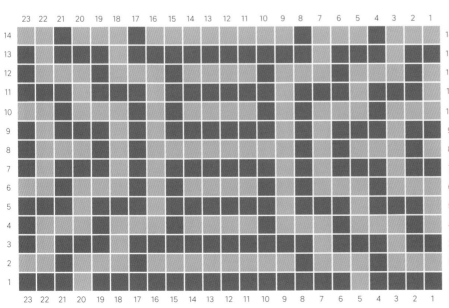

Narwhal School

Claddagh

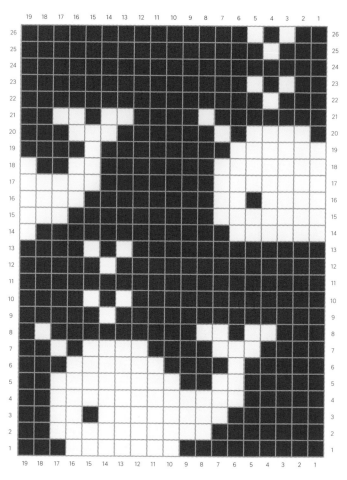

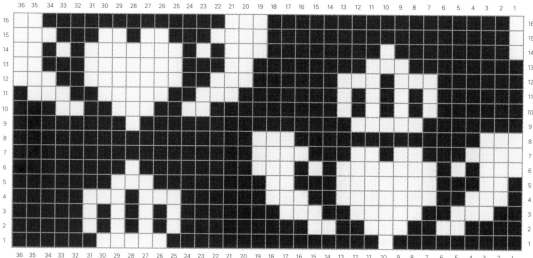

Big Flora

Pieced

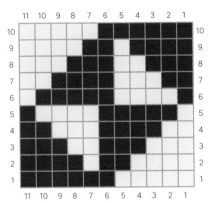

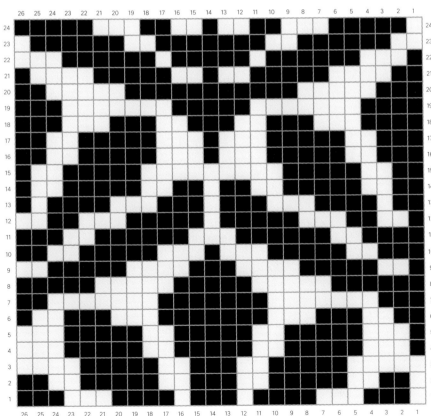

Dotty

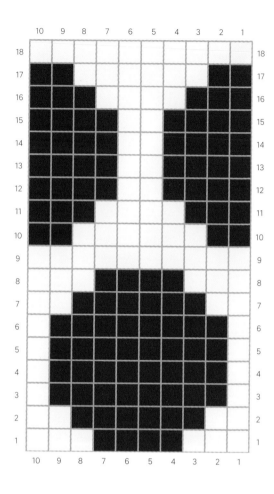

Broken Zigs

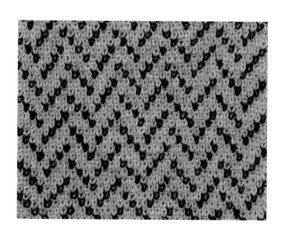

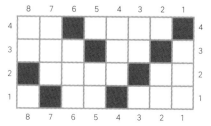

Spring!

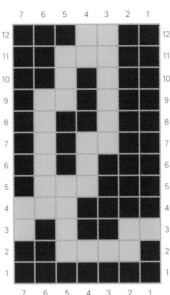

Filigree

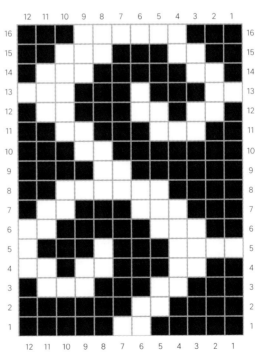

Floating Bows

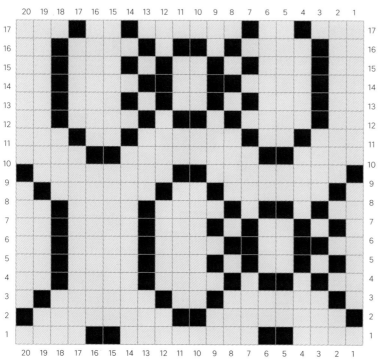

Honeycomb

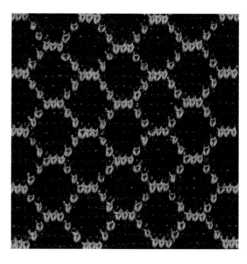

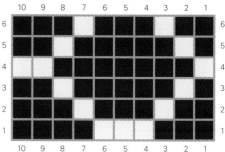

Tip

It really helps to intentionally work the SESC stitch pattern a little more loosely than usual. Pull up just a bit more on your loops as you draw them through the stitch. It will then be much easier to get your hook into the stitches.

Inlaid

Mermaid Scales

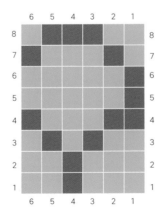

Leafy

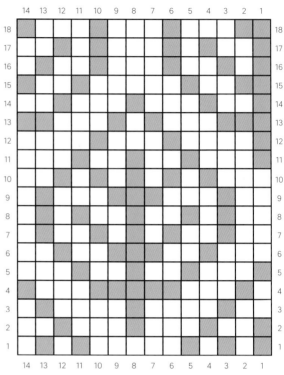

Martini

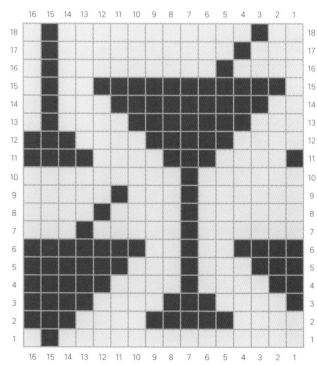

Ninjas

Tip

When working the SESC stitch pattern I use the middle finger of my left hand to feel the back of each stitch as my hook goes through it, to make sure I insert my hook under that horizontal strand.

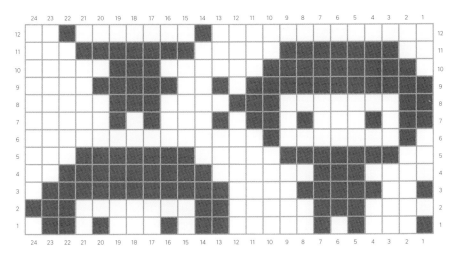

Meow!

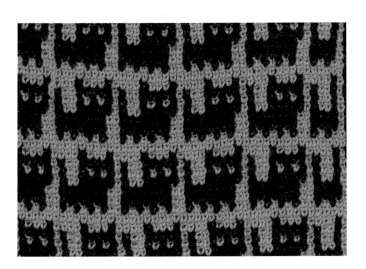

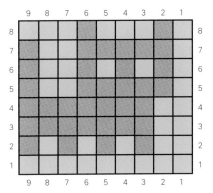

Labyrinth

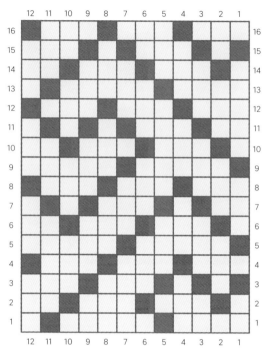

New Growth

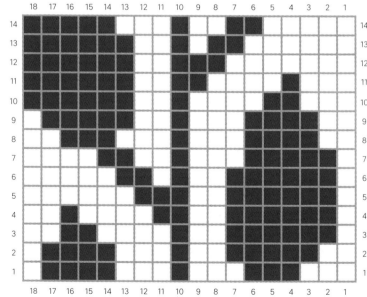

Faded

Snips

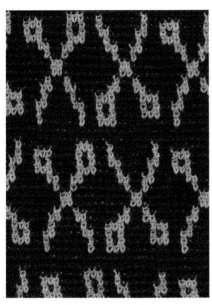

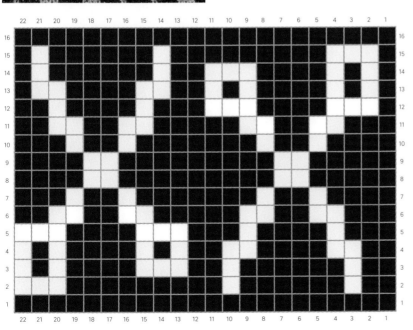

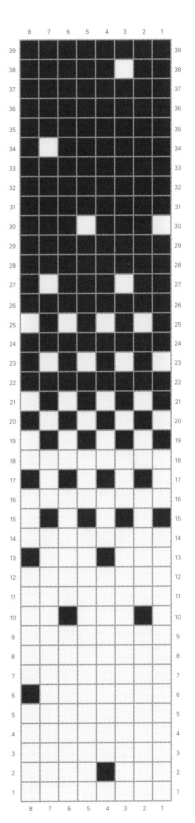

The Projects

These five projects were designed to be timeless patterns that that can be made over and over—customized each time with a new colorwork pattern. See Swapping and Modifying Charts and Project Substitutions for help and information on customization.

Tread Scarf

This is the perfect project for those who are new to colorwork—you don't need to think about shaping, sizing or anything complicated while you watch the pattern form beneath your fingers. The stitch pattern featured here is simple, involves relatively few color changes, and it's easy to keep track of where you are. However, swapping out the stitch pattern for something else is particularly easy for this project (see Swapping And Modifying Charts).

Finished size: 72in (183cm) long x 11in (28cm) wide.

Yarn: Berroco Ultra Alpaca Light (50% superfine alpaca, 50% Peruvian wool; 146yd/133m per 1¾oz/50g; CYCA #3): #4288 Blueberry Mix (MC); #42189 Barley (CC); 4 skeins each color.

Hook: Size F/5 (3.75mm). Adjust hook size if necessary to obtain correct gauge. Getting the exact gauge isn't super important here—it is more important to achieve a fabric with a nice drape. However, the gauge will affect the finished size of your scarf and it may change yarn requirements.

Notions: Stitch markers (optional); yarn needle; piece of cardboard about 7½in (19cm) wide (for making the fringe).

Gauge (tension): 16 sts x 14 rows = 4 x 4in (10 x 10cm) working ESC colorwork pattern using F/5 (3.75mm) hook.

This scarf is constructed in rows with the right side always facing, which means that you will cut your yarn at the end of each row leaving a long yarn tail that later gets incorporated into the fringe. If you want to unravel your swatch in order to re-use that yarn, I recommend making a swatch in the round (and not cutting the yarn) as in Gauge Swatch Directions.

Why I chose this yarn

For this project, I really wanted to show off the same yarn that I used for all of the swatches in this book; to show how it looks in a larger piece being worn on the body. This alpaca and wool mix is lovely and soft, and lends so much drape and warmth—and it comes in a really wide range of colors. It was the perfect choice for this generous scarf!

Gauge swatch directions

Ch 33 sts.

Round 1: Being careful not to twist the chain, beg 2nd ch from hook, ESC in each st across. (32 sts)

Do not join, but continue to work in a spiral. PM to keep track of first st of round.

Rounds 2–14: Work next 13 rounds from chart in ESC stitch pattern, working four reps in each round (see Working From the Colorwork Chart).

Notes

The scarf is worked sideways in rows with right side always facing. Leave 8in (20cm) yarn tails at the beginning and end of every row. These will be incorporated into the fringe later so you will not have to weave in ends (except for any yarn joins). Even though some rows do not require color changes, continue to work over a strand of the opposite color of yarn to maintain an even gauge throughout the scarf. As an added bonus, you can pull on these strands to tighten the edges of the scarf if they become wavy or stretched.

Working from the colorwork chart

Because we are working in rows with the right side always facing, you will follow each line in the chart from right to left. If you crochet left handed, you can follow the chart from left to right. Row 1 of the chart corresponds to Row 1 of the scarf.

When working from the chart, carry the non-working color along the top edge of your stitches from the previous row. Crochet around the non-working yarn encasing it with your stitches. As you work make sure that the yarn you are carrying does not constrict your stitches. Every few stitches after a color change, pull on the end of the carried yarn, so that you know it is not too loose, then pull on the fabric so that you know it is not too tight. When you need to change colors drop the working yarn and pick up the yarn you have been carrying along. Always change to the new color on the last yo of the last stitch before the color change in the chart. As you drop one yarn to pick up the other, drop MC to the front and CC to the back so that you can avoid twisting up your yarn as you work.

This photo shows the wrong side of the Tread Scarf, which also looks great!

SCARF PATTERN

Using MC, ch 292.

TIP: this is a lot of chains to keep track of. If you get lost and add a few extra, you can unravel some after you make your first row and get a chance to count your stitches again. If you mark every 25th or 50th chain with a stitch marker it will be easier to keep track of how many you have already made.

Set-up row: Cont with MC, working into bottom of ch and over strand of CC, ESC in 2nd ch from hook and each ch to end. (291 sts)

Fasten off and cut yarn leaving 8in (20cm) yarn tails at end of row now and throughout pattern. Do not turn.

Rows 1–24: Leave approx. 8in (20cm) beg yarn tails now and throughout rest of pattern (these will be incorporated into fringe). Keeping same side facing, and working over a strand of CC, insert hook in first ESC of set-up row (not beg ch), yo with MC and pull up a loop, ch 2 (does not count as st now and throughout), ESC in same st as beg ch, beg with Row 1 of Chart work in ESC stitch pattern across next 288 sts until 2 sts rem, 1 ESC in rem 2 sts in MC, fasten off leaving 8in (20cm) tail. (291 sts, 36 chart reps, [ch-2 beg chain, 1 ESC] in MC at beg of row, 2 ESC in MC at end of row). Do not turn.

Rows 25–37: Rep Rows 1–13.

Row 38: Join yarn as established and work ch 2 beg ch. Beg with same st, and cont to work over a strand of CC, ESC across row using MC (291 sts)

Fasten off leaving 8in (20cm) tail.

FINISHING

Fasten off. Weave in ends. Block.

FRINGE

For one end of scarf: Wrap the yarn loosely around the 7½in (19cm) piece of cardboard 80 times, then cut through the loops of yarn at one side to create 80 pieces of fringe that measure about 18in (45cm) long. Fasten 20 sections of fringe along each end of the scarf—this means that there will be a section of fringe added into every other row end. Each of the 20 sections are made up of four strands of fringe (held together) and attached as follows: Insert the hook from the WS to the RS through the end of the scarf. Take four pieces of fringe, fold them in half to find the center, and lay the center over the hook. Pull hook through just far enough so that you can get two fingers through the loop. Reach through loop with your fingers and grab the eight ends of yarn and any nearby yarn tails leftover from crocheting the scarf, and pull them through the loop. Pull tightly to secure the fringe. Repeat for each of the remaining fringe sections along the edge.

Repeat the Fringe directions at the opposite end of the scarf. Trim the fringe evenly so that it measures about 6in (15cm) long.

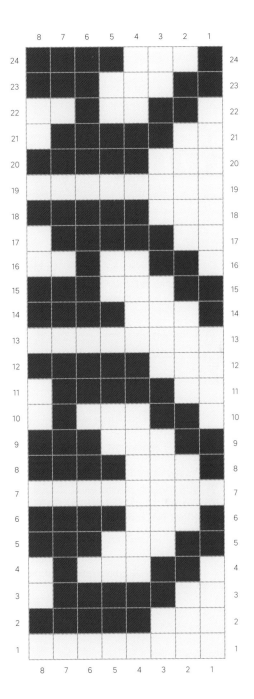

CHART KEY

Each square represents 1 stitch.

Read the chart from right to left (Lefties: from left to right).

Snowy Picture Hat

Remember back in the olden times when your TV had a snowy picture due to bad reception? Sometimes you could just baaarely make out what was happening. Here is a little nod to those simpler times... I love the way that the speckled yarn obscures the image of the television just a little—but you can still tell what it is. It's always important to have enough contrast between your yarns (or the charted image won't show up) but if you use a speckled or ombre yarn where the colors match, every-once-in-a-while it can have a really cool effect!

Finished size: To fit average size woman/teen; 19in (48cm) circumference at ribbed edge x 10½in (26.5cm) tall after blocking.

Yarn: Malabrigo Mechita (100% superwash merino wool; 420yd/384m per 3½oz/100g; CYCA #1): #MTA052 Paris Night (MC); #MTA729 Double Bass (CC); 1 skein each color.

Hook: Sizes B/1 (2.25 mm) and C/2 (2.75 mm). Adjust hook size if necessary to obtain correct gauge.

Notions: Stitch markers; yarn needle; piece of cardboard about 4½in (11.5cm) wide by 5–6in (12.5–15cm) long (for making pompom).

Gauge (tension): 22.5 sts x 15.5 rows = 4 x 4in (10 x 10cm) working ESC colorwork pattern using C/2 (2.75 mm) hook.

Why I chose this yarn

I needed a very thin one-ply yarn so that I could use a larger chart and achieve a smooth stitch pattern. I chose this yarn mostly because it is sooooo soft and just a joy to work with, but also because it had a speckled yarn option as well as solid colors that would go with it. I really wanted this hat to be easy to wear—like you could just throw it on and it would look good. Thanks to the yarn's uber-drape and softness, this hat delivers!

Notes

This hat is worked from the bottom up. First you will work the ribbing in turned rows, then slip stitch the ends together to form a tube. Stitches are worked around the top of the tube, continuing in joined rounds to the top of the hat.

When changing from one color to the next do not fasten off or cut the yarn, but carry it along the top edge working over it (encasing your stitches).

To work joins: On the last yo of the last stitch of the round, use the color to match the first st of round just made. Make your slip stitch join (to the first st) with the same color.

Color of beginning chains: In this pattern your beginning chains do not count as a stitch. You will need to make your beginning chains in the same color as the first stitch of each round. If the first stitch of the next round is a different color than what is on your hook after the ending join, yo with the new color and pull on the old color yarn tail until the last loop of the old color disappears, make your beginning chains, then make your first stitch (into the same stitch as the join).

Stitch guide

ESC (extended single crochet): Insert hook in next st, yo and pull up a loop, yo and pull through just one loop, yo and pull through two loops.

ModESC2tog (extended single crochet 2 stitches together modified): This is worked over the next two stitches, and decreases your stitch count by one stitch. Insert hook under just the front loop of next st, then insert hook under both loops of foll st (from front to back as normal), yo and pull up a loop, yo and pull through just one loop, yo and pull through two loops.

HAT PATTERN

RIBBING

Using B/1 (2.25mm) hook and MC, ch 14.

Row 1: Beg in 3rd ch from hook and working into bottom of ch, 1 hdc in each ch to end, turn. (12 sts)

Rows 2–96: Ch 2, 1 hdc BLO in each st across, turn. (12 sts)

Seaming row: Ch 1, turn as if to work another row, bring starting edge directly in front of last row worked and sl st edges together working through BLO of each edge. (12 sl sts)

Do not fasten off. Turn work so that sl st seam is on inside.

BODY OF HAT

Set-up round: Ch 1, rotate piece to work into ends of rows as foll: PM to divide ribbing into four sections, work 30 sc in each section. PM in first st of round. (120 sts around ribbing)

Change to C/2 (2.75mm) hook.

Round 1 (colorwork stitch pattern beg): Yo with CC and pull up a loop. Pull on MC yarn tail until last loop of MC disappears but do not cut yarn. Working over color not in use and beg with Round 1 of Chart, work next 34 rounds joining after each round (see Notes: To work joins).

SHAPING FOR CROWN OF HAT

Cont to work over color not in use to help keep decrease sts from getting stretched out, and make sts look more even. It also makes top of hat much sturdier so pompom will not pull hat out of shape. Gently pull on non-working color every so often to help pull in sts and to keep non-working color from peeking through. If there is too much color bleed through, work over a strand of MC instead of CC.

DECREASES:

Round 35: ModESC2tog around, join. (60 sts)

Round 36: ESC around, join.

Round 37: ModESC2tog around, join. (30 sts)

Round 38: ModESC2tog around, join. (15 sts)

Round 39: ModESC2tog 7 times, ESC in last st, join. (8 sts)

Fasten off. Using yarn needle, run yarn tail through front loop of rem 8 sts and pull tight to close top of hat.

FINISHING

Weave in ends. Gently block hat.

CHART KEY

Each square represents 1 stitch.

Read the chart from right to left (Lefties: from left to right).

POMPOM

Cut two pieces of yarn to 16in (40.5cm) and set aside. Wrap the yarn loosely around the cardboard about 350 times. Carefully remove the loops from the cardboard and center them over both 16in (40.5cm) pieces of yarn. Tie both pieces of yarn (held together as one) around the center of the loops in a very tight knot. Use scissors to cut all of the loops of the pompom, being careful not to cut the longer strands that were used to tie it together. Fluff the pompom, and trim the ends into a 3in (7.5cm) ball. Using a yarn needle and the long strands, attach the pompom to the top of the hat.

Claddagh Mittens

Block those chilly breezes with center single crochet! This stitch pattern makes an incredibly warm, thick fabric to keep your hands warm all winter. Forget wearing your heart on your sleeve—now you can wear your heart on your mittens!

Finished size: To fit average size woman's hand; 8½in (21.5cm) circumference not incl thumb; cuff 3in (7.5cm) long; hand 7½in (19cm) long (not including cuff). Directions for lengthening or shortening mittens are included within pattern.

Yarn: Brown Sheep Nature Spun Sport Weight (100% wool; 184yd/168m per 1¾oz/50g; CYCA #2): #N25S Enchanted Forest (MC); #N03S Grey Heather (CC); 1 skein each color—if you lengthen fingertips more than ½in (1cm) you may need more MC. If you lengthen palm and the thumbs by more than ½in (1cm) you may need more CC.

Hook: Sizes C/2 (2.75 mm) and D/3 (3.25 mm). Adjust hook size if necessary to obtain correct gauge.

Notions: Four stitch markers; yarn needle.

Gauge (tension): 19 sts x 24 rounds = 4 x 4in (10 x 10cm) working CSC colorwork pattern using D/3 (3.25 mm) hook.

It is common for your gauge to be slightly tighter with colorwork; you may need to switch to a larger hook to keep your gauge even or you could intentionally work the colorwork section a bit looser to maintain the gauge.

Why I chose this yarn

This cozy yarn is a staple for me. I use it so often because it comes in a gazillion colors and is very easy on the pocketbook, but it has so many other great qualities! It is just the right texture for mittens—it is sturdy enough to keep its shape after wearing them over and over (and it wears well even when they get a little wet), yet it is soft enough so they aren't itchy.

Notes

The cuff is worked sideways in turned rows, then seamed with a row of slip stitches. The mitten is then worked in the round from the cuff to the fingertip, setting aside stitches for the thumb to be worked last. Turning chains do not count as a stitch.

Crochet around the non-working yarn encasing it with your stitches. As you work, make sure that the yarn you are carrying does not constrict your stitches. Every few stitches after a color change, pull on the end of the carried yarn, so that you know it is not too loose, then, pull on the fabric so that you know it is not too tight.

When working the solid color sections of the mitten body, you can choose whether or not to continue to carry the non-working color and crochet around it—even when you are no longer working from a chart. Carrying the yarn helps maintain the gauge as well as making the mitten warmer—however, your mitten will have less stretch. I chose to cut the non-working yarn for the CC section to allow more stretch through the palm, but I continued to carry the non-working yarn throughout the fingertip section for more warmth.

Working from the colorwork chart

Always change to the new color on the last yo of the last stitch before the color change on the chart.

Use 1 chain to begin each round, and join with a slip stitch at the end of each round (neither the ch-1 nor the sl st count as stitches in this pattern).

Stitch guide

CSC (center single crochet): Insert hook between the two legs of the next stitch, yo and pull up loop, yo and pull through both loops on hook.

CSC2tog (center single crochet 2 stitches together): Insert hook between the two legs of the next stitch, yo and pull up a loop, insert hook between the two legs of the following st, yo and pull up a loop, yo and pull through all three loops on hook. One stitch decreased.

Note: On the following round or row, when you are working a CSC or CSC2tog into this decrease stitch, you will insert your hook between both sets of legs in the center of the decrease before making the first yo.

MITTENS PATTERN

CUFF

Using C/2 (2/75mm) hook and MC, ch 20.

Row 1: Beg in 3rd ch from hook and working into bottom of ch, 1 hdc in each ch to end, turn. (18 sts)

Rows 2–26: Ch 2 (does not count as st), 1 hdc BLO in each st, turn. Do not fasten off. (18 sts)

Seam cuff as follows: Fold cuff in half so that last row worked is directly in front of starting ch. Sl st through back loops of each layer (through double thickness) across. Do not fasten off. (12 sts) Leave sl st seam on outside (RS) of work.

RIGHT HAND

Round 1: PM in first st of round and to divide top edge of cuff into four equal sections. Ch 1 (does not count as a st), 10 sc in each section of cuff, sl st to join. (40 sts)

Change to D/3 (3.25mm) hook.

Rounds 2–5: Ch 1 (does not count as st now and throughout), yo with CC1 and pull up loop, pull on MC yarn tail until last ch of MC disappears, lay MC across top edge of work to beg Lower Claddagh Chart. Work all four rounds of Chart remembering to work around non-working color (to encase it).***

Note: Here you can cont to work over non-working color or you can cut MC and just cont with CC.

Round 6: Ch 1, CSC in next 23 sts, 2 CSC in next 2 sts, CSC in next 15 sts, sl st to join. (42 sts)

Rounds 7–8: Ch 1, CSC around, sl st to join.

Round 9: Ch 1, CSC in next 24 sts, 2 CSC in next 2 sts, CSC in next 16 sts, sl st to join. (44 sts)

Rounds 10–11: Ch 1, CSC around, sl st to join.

Round 12: Ch 1, CSC in next 25 sts, 2 CSC in next 2 sts, CSC in next 17 sts, sl st to join. (46 sts)

Rounds 13–14: Ch 1, CSC around, sl st to join.

Round 15: Ch 1, CSC in next 26 sts, 2 CSC in next 2 sts, CSC in next 18 sts, sl st to join. (48 sts)

Rounds 16–18: Ch 1, CSC around, sl st to join.

Note: You can alter the length of the mitten palm here by working more or fewer rounds of CC to make it longer or shorter.

Round 19 (thumbhole round): 1 CSC in next 23 sts, ch 2, skip next 10 sts (for thumbhole), PM in first skipped st, 1 CSC in next 15 sts. (40 sts, not including skipped thumb sts)

Rounds 20–38: Work next 19 rounds of CSC from Upper Claddagh Chart, do not fasten off. (40 sts)

Note: You can add rounds of MC here to make mitten longer. To make it shorter, beg Shaping for Fingertip section earlier by beg decrease sts while working last couple of rounds of Chart. If you have substituted with another chart, this may interfere with colorwork, particularly if image spans entire width of chart in last rounds.

FINGERTIP SHAPING

Note: Here you can cont working over CC yarn or you can cut it and cont with only MC (see Notes).

Round 39: Ch 1, [CSC in next st, CSC2tog, CSC in next 15 sts, CSC2tog] twice. sl st to join. (36 sts)

Round 40: Ch 1, CSC around.

Round 41: Ch 1, [CSC in next st, CSC2tog, CSC in next 13 sts, CSC2tog] twice, sl st to join. (32 sts)

Round 42: Ch 1, [CSC in next st, CSC2tog, CSC in next 11 sts, CSC2tog] twice, sl st to join. (28 sts)

Round 43: Ch 1, [CSC in next st, CSC2tog, CSC in next 9 sts, CSC2tog] twice, sl st to join. (24 sts)

Round 44: Ch 1, [CSC in next st, CSC2tog, CSC in next 7 sts, CSC2tog] twice, sl st to join. (20 sts)

Fasten off leaving long tail of MC for closing top of mitten.

THUMB

Pull up loop of MC in marked st (first skipped st of thumb), ch 1, 1 CSC in next 10 sts, 1 ESC in side edge of st where thumb meets hand, 1 CSC in bottom of next 2 ch (made in thumbhole round), 1 ESC in side edge of st where thumb meets hand, do not join. (14 sts)

Next 10 rounds: 1 CSC in each st. (14 sts)

Note: Work more or fewer rounds here to lengthen or shorten thumb.

Next round: CSC2tog 7 times. (7 sts)

Next Round: CSC in each st. (7 sts)

Fasten off leaving long tail. Using yarn needle, weave yarn tail through front loop of rem 7 sts and pull tight to close top of thumb. Using yarn needle and beg yarn tail for thumb, sew closed any holes where thumb meets hand.

LEFT HAND

Work as for Right Hand to ***, then work as foll:

Note: Here you can continue to work over non-working color or you can cut MC and just cont with CC.

Round 6: Ch 1, CSC in next 16 sts, 2 CSC in next 2 sts, CSC in next 22 sts, sl st to join. (42 sts)

Rounds 7–8: Ch 1, CSC around, sl st to join.

Round 9: Ch 1, CSC in next 17 sts, 2 CSC in next 2 sts, CSC in next 23 sts, sl st to join. (44 sts)

Rounds 10–11: Ch 1, CSC around, sl st to join.

Round 12: Ch 1, CSC in next 18 sts, 2 CSC in next 2 sts, CSC in next 24 sts, sl st to join. (46 sts)

Rounds 13–14: Ch 1, CSC around, sl st to join.

Round 15: Ch 1, CSC in next 19 sts, 2 CSC in next 2 sts, CSC in next 25 sts, sl st to join. (48 sts)

Rounds 16–18: Ch 1, CSC around, sl st to join.

Note: You can alter length of mitten palm by working more or fewer rounds of CC here to make it longer or shorter.

Round 19 (thumbhole round): 1 CSC in next 16 sts, ch 2, skip next 10 sts (for thumbhole), PM in first skipped st, 1 CSC in next 22 sts. (40 sts not including skipped thumb sts)

Repeat Directions as for Right Hand beg at Round 20. Work Thumb as for Right Hand.

FINISHING

Using yarn tail and yarn needle, whip stitch the top of mitten closed. Use yarn tail at beginning of thumb to sew closed the small hole where thumb meets hand. Weave in all ends, block.

Lower Claddagh Chart

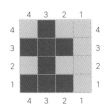

Upper Claddagh Chart

CHART KEY

Each square represents 1 stitch.

Read the chart from right to left (Lefties: make a mirror image copy of the chart (flip it horizontally) and then work it from left to right).

Badlands Cardigan

This is the kind of cardigan I imagine myself in when I daydream about staying in a National Park Lodge. I'm a tent-camping kind of girl, but I fantasize about lounging around in this rustic but classy sweater in front of a giant fireplace after a long day's hike. It's constructed so it's easy to alter: first the colorwork sections are worked so you can check the fit. The body and sleeves are worked top down, so you can adjust the length. Then all three pieces are joined and the yoke is worked from the bottom up so that you can adjust the shoulders if needed later.

Finished size: S, M, L, XL, 2X; sized for 34½ (39, 44, 47¾, 54)in/87.5 (99, 112, 121.5, 137)cm bust. Fit is average/close. Sample is shown in Medium worn with 3½in (9cm) of ease.

Yarn: Jamieson's Double Knitting, (100% Shetland Wool; 82yd/75m per ⅞oz/25g; CYCA #3); #235 Grouse, 22 (24, 28, 30, 34) balls (MC); #230 Yellow Ochre, 6 (6, 7, 8, 9) balls (CC).

Hook: Sizes G/6 (4mm), E/4 (3.5mm) and D/3 (3.25mm). Adjust hook size if necessary to obtain correct gauge.

Notions: Six stitch markers; yarn needle; Six 1⅛in (3cm) buttons (I used LaMode #02908); sewing needle and thread for attaching buttons.

Gauge (tension): 15.5 sts x 19 rounds = 4 x 4in (10 x 10cm) working CSC colorwork pattern using G/6 (4mm) hook.
20.5 sts x 19 rows = 4 x 4in (10 x 10cm) working linen stitch pattern using E/4 (3.5mm) hook.
23 sts x 13 rows = 4 x 4in (10 x 10cm) working hdc BLO pattern using D/3 (3.25mm) hook.

Why I chose this yarn

This is a classic woolen-spun yarn, which means that the fibers are going every-which-way making this a light, rustic, and sticky yarn (the fibers catch on each other and resist slipping out of place). All of these traits make it the perfect yarn for steeking. Also, the linen stitch pattern tends to stretch quite a bit vertically, and I didn't want a heavy yarn that would make the sweater sag—instead this yarn has lots of bounce and blocks so nicely into shape.

Badlands body chart sizes S (L, 2X)

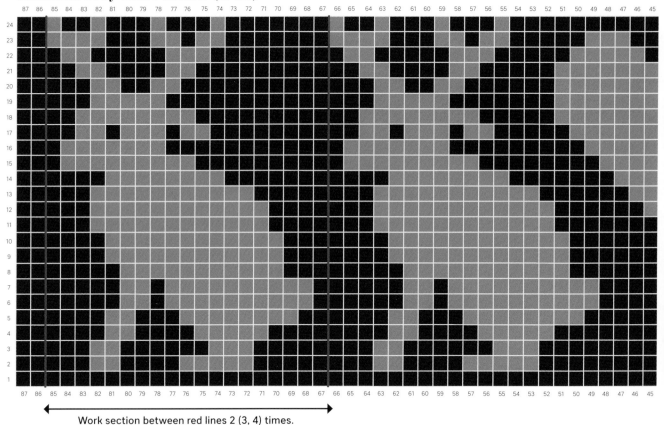

Work section between red lines 2 (3, 4) times.

Notes

Work the colorwork section loosely—it makes it so much easier to get your hook through the stitches.

The ribbing is intentionally worked at a tight gauge to help it keep its shape.

When working ribbing, ch 2 tightly for the turning chain for a neater edge. You will not need to work into these chain stitches so it doesn't matter if they are tight.

See the Steeking Without Freaking! section before beginning this pattern to familiarize yourself with the process of making a crocheted steek.

Stitch guide

WBS (Work Beginning Steek—worked at beg of each round just before working sts from colorwork chart): CSC with MC in first st of previous round changing to CC on last yo, CSC with CC in foll st changing to MC on last yo, CSC with MC in next st changing color on last yo if needed in order to work foll ch-1 in same color as first st of chart, ch 1 with color to be used on foll st (first st of colorwork chart). Now beg to work across chart.

WES (Work Ending steek—worked at end of each round just after working across sts in chart): Change to MC on last yo of last CSC from chart if necessary, ch 1 with MC, CSC with MC in next st changing to CC on last yo, CSC with CC in foll st changing to MC on last yo, CSC with MC in next st making last yo with BOTH yarns held together as one, cont with both yarns held together as one, ch 2, drop CC, ch 1 with MC.

Linen dec (linen stitch decrease in single crochet—working first leg of decrease into next ch-1 sp and 2nd leg into foll ch-1 sp: Insert hook into next ch-1 sp, yo and pull up a loop, insert hook in foll ch-1 sp, yo and pull up loop, yo and pull through all 3 loops (2 sts decreased).

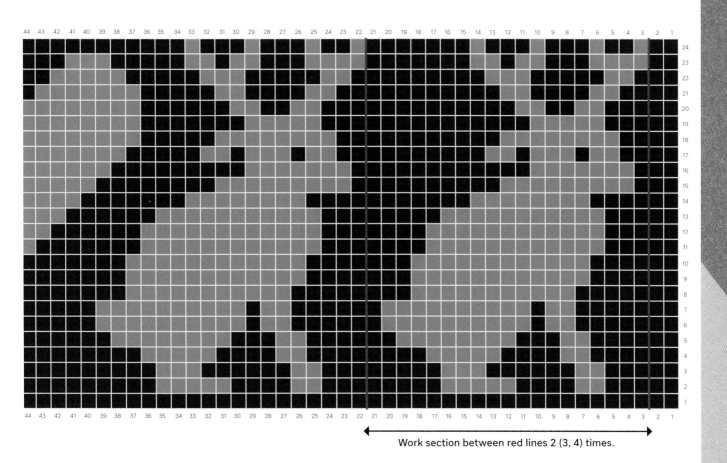

Work section between red lines 2 (3, 4) times.

CARDIGAN PATTERN

BODY

Work 125 (143, 163, 177, 201) sts from Badlands Body Chart in correct size, working CSC in round with ch-3 steek as follows:

Using G/6 (4mm) hook and MC, ch 134 (152, 172, 186, 210).

Round 1: Beg in 2nd ch from hook and working in bottom of ch, sc in next 3 ch, PM in first st of round, ch 1, sc in each ch until 4 ch rem, ch 1, sc in next 2 ch, sc in last ch making last yo with MC and CC held together (to add CC yarn), ch 2 (with both strands of yarn), drop color not needed in first steek st of next round, ch 1 with rem color, do not join, but work in a spiral. First st of foll round will be made in first (marked) st of this round. (125 (143, 163, 177, 201) colorwork sts, with a ch-1 sp and 3 steek sts ON EACH END separated by 3 ch)

Round 2: From this point onward, work in rounds without joins. First st of this round is made in first st of Round 1; be careful not to twist Round 1 and remember to work over non-working yarn as you create steek and colorwork section. WBS, work across Badlands Body Chart Round 2, WES. (125 (143, 163, 177, 201) sts + 11 sts of steek)

Rounds 3–24: WBS, work across chart, WES.

Fasten off.

Place contrast marker in first st, PM in each st as foll:
26th, 31st, 95th, 100th for Size S.
31st, 36th, 108th, and 113th sts for Size M.
36th, 41st, 123rd, and 128th sts for Size L.
40th, 45th, 133rd, and 138th sts for Size XL.
46th, 52nd, 150th, and 156th sts for Size 2X.

Reinforce and cut steek (see Steeking Without Freaking! section).

Rotate colorwork section 180 degrees to work across bottom edge. Only work across sts from chart—do not work steek sts.

Change to D/3 (3.25mm) hook.

Badlands body chart sizes M (XL)

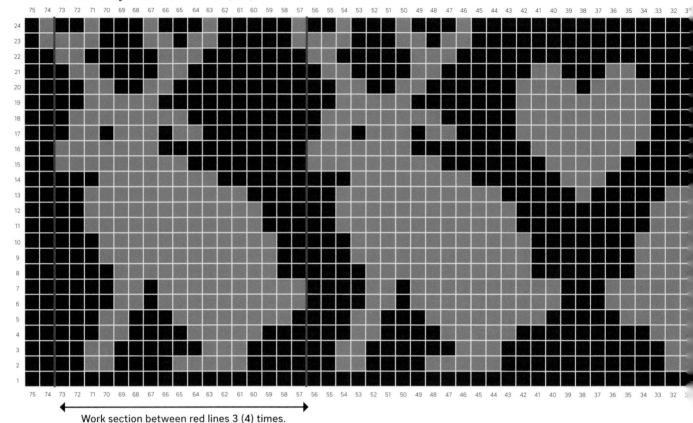

Work section between red lines 3 (4) times.

Row 1 (RS): [2 sc in next st, sc in next 2 sts], across until 2 (2, 1, 3, 3) sts rem, 2 (2, 1, 1, 1) sc in next st, 1 sc in next 1 (1, 0, 2, 2) sts. (167 (191, 217, 235, 267) sc sts across colorwork bottom edge)

Change to E/4 (3.5mm) hook.

Row 2 (WS): Ch 1, turn, [sc in next st, ch 1, skip next st] across until 1 st rem, sc in last st. (167 (191, 217, 235, 267) sts)

Change to CC.

Row 3 (RS): Ch 1, turn, sl st BLO in next st, [sc in next ch sp, ch 1] across until 2 sts rem, sc in next ch-1 sp, sl st BLO in last st. (167 (191, 217, 235, 267) sts)

Row 4: Ch 1, turn, sc in next st, ch1, [sc in next ch-1 sp, ch 1] across until 1 st rem, sc in last st. (167 (191, 217, 235, 267) sts)

Change to MC.

Rows 5–8: Rep Rows 3 and 4 twice more. Change to CC.

Rows 9–12: Rep Rows 3 and 4 twice more. Change to MC.

Row 13: Rep Row 3.

Row 14: Rep Row 4.

Row 15: Ch 1, turn, sl st BLO in next st, [sc in next ch sp, ch 1] 18 (21, 24, 26, 30) times, [sc, ch 1] twice in next ch-1 sp, [sc in next ch sp, ch 1] across until 19 (22, 25, 27, 31) ch-1 sps rem, [sc, ch 1] twice in next ch-1 sp, [sc in next ch sp, ch 1] across until 2 sts rem, sc in next ch-1 sp, sl st BLO in last st (4 sts increased, 171 (195, 221, 239, 271) sts)

Rows 16–23: Rep Rows 3 and 4 four more times.

Row 24 (WS): Rep Row 3 once more.

Rows 25–34: Rep Rows 15–24. (175 (199, 225, 243, 275) sts)

Rows 35–44: Rep Rows 15–24. (179 (203, 229, 247, 279) sts)

Rows 45–46 (45–46, 45–48, 45–48, 45-50): Rep Rows 3 and 4 once (once, twice, twice, three times) more, ending with WS row. Do not fasten off.

RIBBING

Change to D/3 (3.25mm) hook. Make ribbing at same time as working across bottom of last row of body as foll:

Row 1: Ch 12, beg in 3rd ch from hook, working in bottom of ch, 1 hdc in each ch to end. (10 sts)

Row 2: Skip first st along bottom edge, sl st in next 3 sts of bottom row (sl sts do not count as sts), turn to work 1 hdc BLO in each hdc of ribbing. (10 sts)

Row 3: Ch 2, turn, hdc BLO across ribbing. (10 sts)

Row 4: Sl st in next 3 sts of bottom row (sl sts do not count as sts), turn to work 1 hdc BLO in each hdc of ribbing. (10 sts)

Rep Rows 3–4 across bottom edge of sweater until either:
One st rem: sl st in last st. Fasten off.
Two sts rem: sl st in next 2 sts of bottom row (sl sts do not count as sts), turn to work 1 hdc BLO in each hdc of ribbing. Fasten off.
Three sts rem: Rep Row 4, then Row 3. Fasten off.

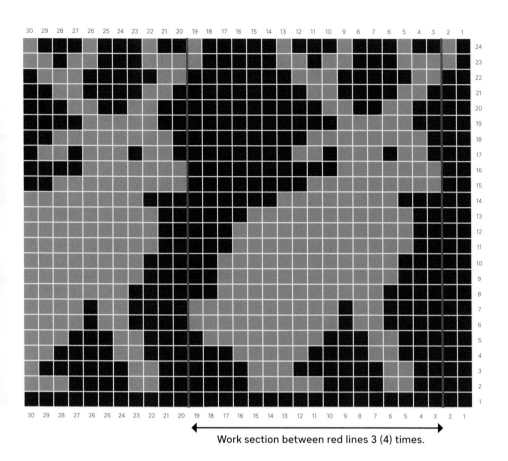

Work section between red lines 3 (4) times.

TIP: The ribbing should be the same width as the bottom
edge of the linen stitch pattern. If you notice that the
ribbing is rippling or flaring outward, when working
the slip sts along the bottom edge of the sweater, try
skipping the first stitch and making a slip stitch in each
of the following three stitches every so often to keep the
ribbing edge straight.

Badlands right sleeve chart size S

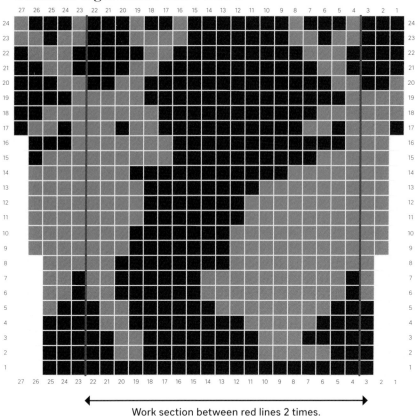

Work section between red lines 2 times.

CHART KEY

Each colored square represents 1 stitch.

For RIGHT sleeve, read the chart from right to left (Lefties: read the chart from left to right).

For LEFT sleeve, copy the chart and flip it horizontally or read it in a mirror, then read it from right to left as normal. (Lefties: copy and flip the chart as above but read the chart from left to right.)

SLEEVES

RIGHT SLEEVE COLORWORK BAND

Using G/6 (4mm) hook and MC, ch 42 (48, 54, 58, 66), sl st in first st to join being careful not to twist ch.

Round 1: Sc in each st, do not join from this point, work in a spiral, PM in bottom of last sc (in foundation ch). (42 (48, 54, 58, 66) sts)

Rounds 2-7 (2-7, 2-7, 2-6, 2-6): Work next 7 (7, 7, 6, 6) rounds from Badlands Right Sleeve Chart in correct size, using CSC stitch pattern.

Rounds 8 (8, 8, 7, 7): Cont working from chart, 2 CSC in first st, CSC around, 2 CSC in last st (44 (50, 56, 60, 68) sts)

Rounds 9-15 (9-15, 9-15, 8-12, 8-12): Cont working from chart in CSC stitch patttern.

Round 16 (16, 16, 13, 13): Cont working from chart, 2 CSC in first st, CSC around, 2 CSC in last st (46 (52, 58, 62, 70) sts)

Rounds 17-24 (17-24, 17-24, 14-18, 14-18): Cont working from chart in CSC stitch pattern.

SIZES XL AND 2X ONLY

Round 19: Cont to work from Badlands Right Sleeve Chart in correct size, 2 CSC in first st, CSC around, 2 CSC in last st (64 (72) sts)

Rounds 20-24: Cont working from chart in CSC stitch pattern.

SIZES S, M, L, AND XL ONLY

Fasten off. Place contrast marker in 3rd st of round, PM in 44th (50th, 56th, 62nd) st of round. (4 sts between markers at underarm).

SIZE 2X ONLY

Fasten off.

For Right Sleeve: Place contrast marker in 3rd st of round, PM in 69th st of round.

For Left Sleeve: Place contrast marker in 4th st of round, PM in 70th st of round. (5 sts between markers at underarm).

LOWER RIGHT SLEEVE

Rotate sleeve to work in bottom edge of foundation ch (colorwork down to cuff). Change to D/3 (3.25mm) hook.

Row 1: Pull up loop in marked st of foundation ch, ch 1 (does not count as a st], [2 sc in next st, sc in next 2 sts], until 3 (3, 3, 4, 3) sts rem, 2 sc in next st, sc in next 1 (1, 1, 2, 1) sts, 2 (2, 2, 1, 2) sc in last st, turn, do not join but work in turned rows. (57 (65, 73, 77, 89) sts)

Note: The lower sleeves are worked in turned rows and seamed. This avoids stretching and simplifies the stitches (joining in this stitch pattern can be confusing). If you prefer sleeves without seams, work in joined, turned rounds to keep the stitch pattern consistent with the body. Use a stitch marker to keep track of first stitch of each round."

Change to E/4 (3.5mm) hook.

Row 2 (WS): Ch 1 (turning ch does not count as a st now and throughout), [sc in next st, skip next st, ch 1] across until 1 st rem, sc in last st changing to CC in last yo, turn. (57 (65, 73, 77, 89) sts)

Badlands right sleeve chart size M

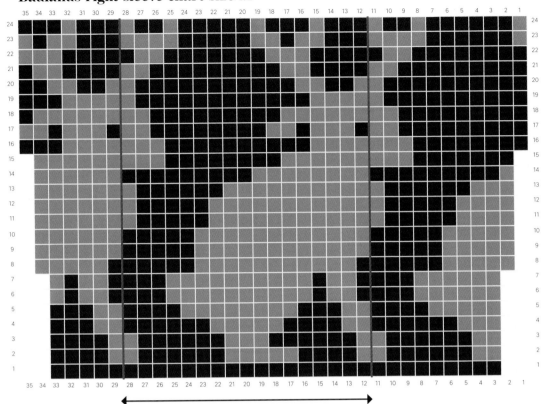

Work section between red lines 2 times.

SIZES S (M) ONLY

Row 3 (RS): Ch 1, sl st BLO in first st, [sc in next ch-1 sp, ch 1] across until 1 st rem, sl st BLO in last st, turn (57 (65) sts)

SIZES L, XL AND 2X ONLY

Row 3 (RS): Ch 1, sl st BLO in first st, linen dec, ch 1, [sc in next ch-1 sp, ch 1] across until two ch-1 spaces rem, linen dec, sl st BLO in last st, turn. (69 (73, 85) sts)

ALL SIZES

Row 4: Ch 1, sc in next ch st, ch 1, [sc in next ch-1 sp, ch 1] across until 1 st rem, sc in last sl st of row changing to MC in last yo, turn. (57 (65, 69, 73, 85) sts)

Row 5 (RS): Ch 1, sl st BLO in first st, [sc in next ch-1 sp, ch 1] across until 1 st rem, sl st BLO in last st, turn.

Row 6: Ch 1, sc in next ch st, ch 1, [sc in next ch-1 sp, ch 1] across until 1 st rem, sc in last sl st, turn.

Row 7 (RS): Rep Row 5.

Row 8: Ch 1, sc in next ch st, ch 1, [sc in next ch-1 sp, ch 1] across until 1 st rem, sc in last sl st of row changing to CC in last yo, turn. (57 (65, 69, 73, 85) sts)

SIZES S, M AND L ONLY

Row 9: (RS): Rep Row 5.

Row 10: Rep Row 6.

Row 11 (RS): Rep Row 5.

Row 12: Ch 1, sc in next ch st, ch 1, [sc in next ch-1 sp, ch 1] across until 1 st rem, sc in last sl st of row changing to MC in last yo, turn. (57 (65, 69) sts)

Row 13 (RS): Ch 1, sl st BLO in first st, linen dec, ch 1, [sc in next ch 1 sp, ch 1] across until 2 ch-1 sps rem, linen dec, sl st BLO in last st, turn. (53 (61, 65) sts)

Rows 14: Rep Row 6.

Row 15: Rep Row 5.

Rows 16–23: Rep Rows 14–15 four more times.

Row 24: Rep Row 14.

Rows 25–48: Rep Rows 13–24 twice more. (45 (53, 57) sts)

Do not fasten off.

Badlands right sleeve chart size L

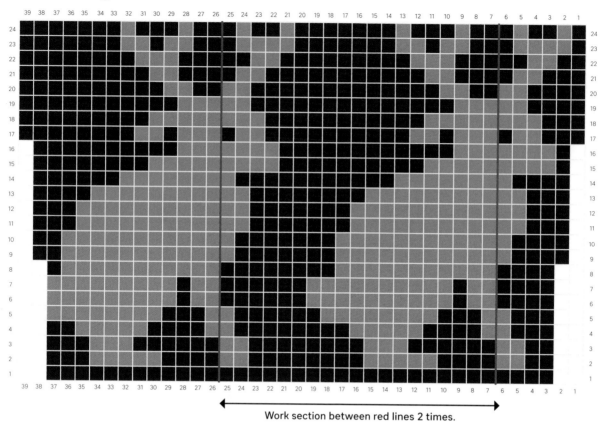

Work section between red lines 2 times.

Badlands right sleeve chart size XL

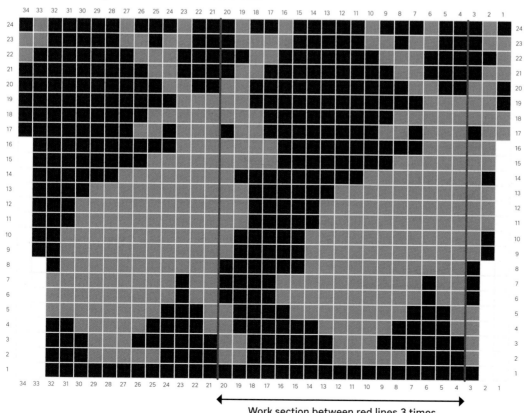

Work section between red lines 3 times.

CHART KEY

Each colored square represents 1 stitch.

For RIGHT sleeve, read the chart from right to left (Lefties: read the chart from left to right).

For LEFT sleeve, copy the chart and flip it horizontally or read it in a mirror, then read it from right to left as normal. (Lefties: copy and flip the chart as above but read the chart from left to right.)

Badlands right sleeve chart size 2X

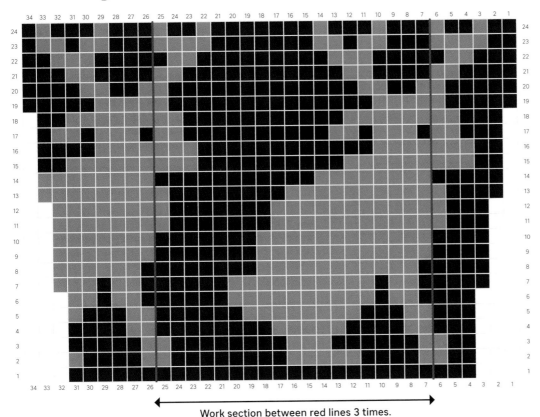

Work section between red lines 3 times.

SIZE S ONLY
Cont with Sleeve Ribbing.

SIZES M AND L ONLY
Row 49: Rep Row 13. (49 (53) sts)

Row 50: Rep Row 14.

SIZE XL ONLY
Row 9: Rep Row 5.

Row 10: Rep Row 6.

Row 11 (RS): Ch 1, sl st BLO in first st, linen dec, ch 1, [sc in next ch-1 sp, ch 1] across until 2 ch-1 sps rem, linen dec, sl st BLO in last st, turn. (69 sts)

Row 12: Ch 1, sc in next ch st, ch 1, [sc in next ch-1 sp, ch 1] across until 1 st rem, sc in last sl st of row changing to MC in last yo, turn.

Rows 13–18: Rep Rows 5 and 6 three times.

Rows 19 (RS): Ch 1, sl st BLO in first st, linen dec, ch 1, [sc in next ch-1 sp, ch 1] across until 2 ch-1 sps rem, linen dec, sl st BLO of last st, turn. (65 sts)

Rows 20: Rep Row 6.

Rows 21–26: Rep Rows 5 and 6 three more times.

Rows 27–50: Rep Rows 19-26 three more times. (53 sts)

Rows 51–52: Rep Rows 5 and 6.

SIZE 2X ONLY
Row 9: Ch 1, sl st BLO in first st, linen dec, ch 1, [sc in next ch-1 sp, ch 1] across until 2 ch-1 sps rem, linen dec, sl st BLO in last st, turn. (81 sts)

Row 10: Rep Row 6.

Row 11 (RS): Rep Row 5.

Row 12: Ch 1, sc in next ch st, ch 1, [sc in next ch-1 sp, ch 1] across until 1 st rem, sc in last sl st of row changing to MC in last yo, turn.

Row 13: Rep Row 5.

Row 14: Rep Row 6.

Row 15: Ch 1, sl st BLO in first st, linen dec, ch 1, [sc in next ch-1 sp, ch 1] across until 2 ch-1 sps rem, linen dec, sl st BLO in last st, turn. (77 sts)

Row 16: Rep Row 6.

Row 17 (RS): Rep Row 5.

Rows 18–19: Rep Rows 16 and 17.

Row 20: Rep Row 6.

Rows 21-50: Rep Rows 15–20 five more times. (57 sts at end)

Row 51: Rep Row 6. (57 sts)

Row 52: Rep Row 5.

SLEEVE RIBBING

Change to D/3 (3.25mm) hook. Make ribbing at same time as working across bottom of last row of sleeve.

Row 1: Ch 18, beg in 3rd ch from hook, working in bottom of ch, 1 hdc in each ch to end. (16 sts)

Row 2: Skip first st from bottom edge of sleeve, sl st in next 3 sts of bottom row (sl sts do not count as sts), rotate to work 1 hdc BLO in each hdc of ribbing. (16 sts)

Row 3: Ch 2, turn, hdc BLO across ribbing. (16 sts)

Row 4: Sl st in next 3 sts of bottom row (sl sts do not count as sts), rotate to work 1 hdc BLO in each st of ribbing. (16 sts)

Rep Rows 3–4 across bottom edge of sleeve until either:
One st rem: Sl st in last st.
Two sts rem: Sl st in next 2 sts of bottom row (sl sts do not count as sts), turn to work 1 hdc BLO in each hdc of ribbing.
Three sts rem: Rep Row 4, then Row 3.

Fasten off leaving long tail for sewing sleeve seam.

LEFT SLEEVE

Work as for Right Sleeve but first copy the Badlands Right Sleeve Chart in the correct size and flip it horizontally, or read it in a mirror, then read it from right to left as normal. (Lefties: copy and flip the chart as above but read the chart from left to right.)

SWEATER UPPER/YOKE

To join sleeves to body use D/3 (3.25mm) and MC and work [2 sc in next st, 1 sc in the next 2 sts] pattern across Right Front, then Right Sleeve, across Back Body, then across Left Sleeve, ending with Left Front as foll:

Row 1 (RS): Using st pattern as above, work across Right Front beg at contrast marker and ending with next marked st of Body, place Right Sleeve next to working loop, beg with contrast marked st work around Sleeve ending with marked st of Sleeve. Cont with next marked st of Body, work across Back body ending with next marked st of Body. Place Left Sleeve next to working loop, beg with contrast marked st work around Sleeve ending with marked st of Sleeve. Cont with next marked st of Body, work across Left Front until 3 (3, 2, 3, 1) sts rem, 2 sc in next 1 (1, 1, 1, 0) sts, sc in next st, 2 sc in next 1 (1, 0, 1, 0) sts. (269 (309, 351, 381, 433) sts around yoke)

Note: Stitch count must be an odd number.

Row 2 (WS): Change to E/4 (3.5mm hook), ch 1 (does not count as st), sc in next ch st, ch 1, [sc in next ch-1 sp, ch 1] across until 1 st rem, sc in last sl st of row, turn (269 (309, 351, 381, 433) sts)

Row 3 (RS): Ch 1, turn, sl st BLO in next st, linen dec, ch 1, [sc in next ch sp, ch 1] 15 (18, 21, 24, 28) times, linen dec, PM in dec, ch 1, [sc in next ch sp, ch 1] 26 (30, 34, 36, 42) times, linen dec, PM in dec, ch 1, [sc in next ch sp, ch 1] 39 (46, 53, 58, 64) times, linen dec, PM in dec, ch 1, [sc in next ch sp, ch 1] 26 (30, 34, 36, 42) times, linen dec, PM in dec, ch 1, [sc in next ch sp, ch 1] 15 (18, 21, 24, 28) times, linen dec, sl st BLO in last st changing to CC on last yo. (12 sts dec, 255 (297, 339, 369, 421) sts)

Note: On WS rows, move markers to ch-1 above marked dec sts.

Row 4 (WS): Ch 1, turn, sc in next st, ch 1, [sc in next ch-1 sp, ch 1] across until 1 st rem, sc in last st. Re-place markers in ch-1 sps.

Row 5 (RS): Ch 1, turn, sl st BLO in next st, linen dec, ch 1, [sc in next ch sp, ch 1] across ending with last sc in ch-1 sp before marked ch-1 sp, linen dec (first leg of dec in marked st), ch 1, [sc in next ch sp, ch 1] across, leaving ch-1 sp BEFORE marked ch-1 sp free, linen dec (2nd leg of dec in marked ch-1 sp), ch 1, [sc in next ch sp, ch 1] across, ending with last sc in sp before marked ch-1 sp, linen dec (first leg of dec in marked ch-1 sp), [sc in next ch sp, ch 1] across leaving ch-1 sp BEFORE marked ch-1 sp free, linen dec (2nd leg of dec in marked ch-1 sp), ch 1, [sc in next ch sp, ch 1] across until 2 ch-1 sps rem, linen dec, sl st BLO in last st changing to MC on last yo. (12 sts dec, 243 (285, 327, 357, 409) sts)

Row 6: Rep Row 4.

Row 7 (RS): Ch 1, turn, sl st BLO in next st, linen dec, ch 1, [sc in next ch sp, ch 1] across leaving ch-1 sp BEFORE marked ch-1 sp free, linen dec (2nd leg of dec in marked ch-1 sp), ch 1, [sc in next ch sp, ch 1] across, ending with last sc in ch-1 sp before marked ch-1 sp, linen dec (first leg of dec in marked st), ch 1, [sc in next ch sp, ch 1] across, leaving ch-1 sp BEFORE marked ch-1 sp free, linen dec (2nd leg of dec in marked ch-1 sp), ch 1, [sc in next ch sp, ch 1] across ending with last sc in sp before marked ch-1 sp, linen dec (first leg of dec in marked ch-1 sp), ch 1, [sc in next ch sp, ch 1] across until 2 ch-1 sps rem, linen dec, sl st BLO in last st changing to MC on last yo. (12 sts dec, 231 (273, 315, 345, 397) sts)

Row 8: Rep Row 4.

Row 9 (RS): Rep Row 5. (219 (261, 303, 333, 385) sts)

Row 10: Ch 1, turn, sc in next st, ch 1, [sc in next ch-1 sp, ch 1] across until 1 st rem, sc in last st changing to CC on last yo.

Row 11 (RS): Rep Row 7. (207 (249, 291, 321, 373) sts)

Row 12: Rep Row 4.

Row 13 (RS): Rep Row 5, changing to MC on last yo. (12 sts decreased, 195 (237, 279, 309, 361) sts)

Cut CC yarn.

Row 14 and all even (WS) rows through Row 40: Rep Row 4.

Row 15 (RS): Rep Row 7. (183 (225, 267, 297, 349) sts)

Row 17 (RS): Ch 1, turn, sl st BLO in next st, [linen dec, ch 1] 0 (1, 1, 1, 1) times, [sc in next ch sp, ch 1] across, ending with last sc in ch-1 sp before marked ch-1 sp, linen dec (first leg of dec in marked st), ch 1, [sc in next ch sp, ch 1] across, leaving ch-1 sp BEFORE marked ch-1 sp free, linen dec (2nd leg of dec in marked ch-1 sp), ch 1, [sc in next ch sp, ch 1] across, ending with last sc in sp before marked ch-1 sp, linen dec (first leg of dec in marked ch-1 sp), [sc in next ch sp, ch 1] across, leaving ch-1 sp BEFORE marked ch-1 sp free, linen dec (2nd leg of dec in marked ch-1 sp), ch 1, [sc in next ch sp, ch 1] across until 0 (2, 2, 2, 2) ch-1 sps rem, [linen dec] 0 (1, 1, 1, 1) times, sl st BLO in last st. (8 (12, 12, 12, 12) sts dec, 175 (213, 255, 285, 337) sts)

Row 19 (RS): Ch 1, turn, sl st BLO in next st, [linen dec, ch 1] 1 (0, 1, 1, 1) times, [sc in next ch sp, ch 1] across, leaving ch-1 sp BEFORE marked ch-1 sp free, linen dec (2nd leg of dec in marked ch-1 sp), ch 1, [sc in next ch sp, ch 1] across, ending with last sc in ch-1 sp before marked ch-1 sp, linen dec (first leg of dec in marked st), ch 1, [sc in next ch sp, ch 1] across, leaving ch-1 sp BEFORE marked ch-1 sp free, linen dec (2nd leg of dec in marked ch-1 sp), ch 1, [sc in next ch sp, ch 1] across, ending with last sc in sp before marked ch-1 sp, linen dec (first leg of dec in marked st), ch 1, [sc in next ch sp, ch 1] across until 2 (0, 2, 2, 2) ch-1 sps rem, [linen dec] 1 (0, 1, 1, 1) times, sl st BLO in last st. (12 (8, 12, 12, 12) sts dec, 163 (205, 243, 273, 325) sts)

Row 21 (RS): Ch 1, turn, sl st BLO in next st, [linen dec, ch 1] 0 (1, 0, 1, 1) times, [sc in next ch sp, ch 1] across ending with last sc in ch-1 sp before marked ch-1 sp, linen dec (first leg of dec in marked st), ch 1, [sc in next ch sp, ch 1] across leaving ch-1 sp BEFORE marked ch-1 sp free, linen dec (2nd leg of dec in marked ch-1 sp), ch 1, [sc in next ch sp, ch 1] across ending with last sc in sp before marked ch-1 sp, linen dec (first leg of dec in marked ch-1 sp), [sc in next ch sp, ch 1] across leaving ch-1 sp BEFORE marked ch-1 sp free, linen dec (2nd leg of dec in marked ch-1 sp), ch 1, [sc in next ch sp, ch 1] across until 0 (2, 0, 2, 2) ch-1 sps rem, [linen dec] 0 (1, 0, 1, 1) times, sl st BLO in last st. (8 (12, 8, 12, 12) sts dec, 155 (193, 235, 261, 313) sts)

Row 23 (RS): Ch 1, turn, sl st BLO in next st, [linen dec, ch 1] 1 (0, 1, 0, 1) times, [sc in next ch sp, ch 1] across leaving ch-1 sp BEFORE marked ch-1 sp free, linen dec (2nd leg of dec in marked ch-1 sp), ch 1, [sc in next ch sp, ch 1] across ending with last sc in ch-1 sp before marked ch-1 sp, linen dec (first leg of dec in marked st), ch 1, [sc in next ch sp, ch 1] across leaving ch-1 sp BEFORE marked ch-1 sp free, linen dec (2nd leg of dec in marked ch-1 sp), ch 1, [sc in next ch sp, ch 1] across ending with last sc in sp before marked ch-1 sp, linen dec (first leg of dec in marked st), ch 1, [sc in next ch sp, ch 1] across until 2 (0, 2, 0, 2) ch-1 sps remain, [linen dec] 1 (0, 1, 0, 1) times, sl st BLO in last st. (12 (8, 12, 8, 12) sts dec, 143 (185, 223, 253, 303) sts)

Row 25 (RS): Ch 1, turn, sl st BLO in next st, [linen dec, ch 1] 0 (1, 0, 1, 0) times, [sc in next ch sp, ch 1] across ending with last sc in ch-1 sp before marked ch-1 sp, linen dec (first leg of dec in marked st), ch 1, [sc in next ch sp, ch 1] across leaving ch-1 sp BEFORE marked ch-1 sp free, linen dec (2nd leg of dec in marked ch-1 sp), ch 1, [sc in next ch sp, ch 1] across ending with last sc in sp before marked ch-1 sp, linen dec (first leg of dec in marked ch-1 sp), [sc in next ch sp, ch 1] across leaving ch-1 sp BEFORE marked ch-1 sp free, linen dec (2nd leg of dec in marked ch-1 sp), ch 1, [sc in next ch sp, ch 1] across until 0 (2, 0, 2, 0) ch-1 sps rem, [linen dec] 0 (1, 0, 1, 0) times, sl st BLO in last st. (8 (12, 8, 12, 8) sts dec, 135 (173, 215, 241, 295) sts)

Row 27 (RS): Rep Row 23. (123 (165, 203, 233, 283) sts)

SIZES M (L, XL, 2X) ONLY
Row 29 (RS): Rep Row 25. (153 (195, 221, 275) sts)

Row 31 (RS): Rep Row 23. (145 (183, 213, 263) sts)

SIZES L (XL, 2X) ONLY
Row 33 (RS): Rep Row 25. (175 (201, 255) sts)

Row 35 (RS): Rep Row 23. (163 (193, 243) sts)

SIZES XL (2X) ONLY
Row 37 (RS): Rep Row 25. (181 (235) sts)

Row 39 (RS): Rep Row 23. (173 (223) sts)

SIZE 2X ONLY
Row 41 (RS): Rep Row 25. (215 sts)

Row 43 (RS): Rep Row 23. (203 sts)

ALL SIZES
Beg shaping for top of shoulders.Remove 1st and 4th markers (that mark front raglan dec lines).

Row 29 (33, 37, 41, 45) (RS): Ch 1, turn, sl st BLO in next st, [linen dec, ch 1] twice, [sc in next ch sp, ch 1] across leaving ch-1 sp BEFORE marked ch-1 sp free, linen dec (2nd leg of dec in marked ch-1 sp), re-place marker in top of this dec st, ch 1, linen dec (do not mark this dec st), ch 1, [sc in next ch sp, ch 1] across leaving two ch-1 sps free before marked ch-1 sp, linen dec, ch 1, linen dec (first leg of dec in marked ch-1 sp), re-place marker in 2nd dec st only, ch 1, [sc in next ch sp, ch 1] across until 4 ch-1 sps rem, linen dec, ch 1, linen dec, sl st BLO in last st. (16 sts dec, 107 (129, 147, 157, 187) sts)

Row 31 (35 39, 43, 47) (RS): Rep Row 29 (33, 37, 41, 45). (91 (113, 131, 141, 171) sts)

Row 33 (37, 41, 45, 49) (RS): Rep Row 29 (33, 37, 41, 45). (75 (97, 115, 125, 155) sts)

Row 35 (39, 43, 47, 51) (RS): Rep Row 29 (33, 37, 41, 45). (59 (81, 99, 109, 139) sts)

SIZE S ONLY

Fasten off.

SIZES M (L, XL, 2X) ONLY

Row 41 (45, 49, 53) (RS): Rep Row 33 (37, 41, 45). (65 (83, 93, 123) sts)

SIZE M, L AND XL ONLY

Fasten off.

SIZE 2X ONLY

Row 55 (RS): Rep Row 45. (107 sts)

Fasten off.

LEFT COLLAR

Using D/3 (3.25mm) hook and MC, ch 46 (48, 50, 52, 56).

Row 1: Beg with 3rd ch from hook and working in bottom of ch, hdc in each ch to end, turn. (44 (46, 48, 50, 54) hdc)

Rows 2–12 (2–14, 2–17, 2–19, 2–20): Ch 2 (doesn't count as a st), hdc BLO to end. (44 (46, 48, 50, 54) hdc BLO)

PM in bottom of same ch in which last hdc of Row 1 was worked. Place contrast marker to mark Row 2 (2, 3, 3, 2) as RS.

Row 13 (15, 18, 20, 21): Ch 2, hdc2tog BLO, hdc BLO to end, turn. (43 (45, 47, 49, 53) sts)

Row 14 (16, 19, 21, 22): Ch 2, hdc BLO across, turn.

Row 15 (17, 20, 22, 23): Ch 2, hdc2tog BLO, hdc BLO to end, turn. (42 (44, 46, 48, 52) sts)

Row 16 (18, 21, 23, 24): Ch 2, hdc BLO across, turn.

Row 17 (19, 22, 24, 25): Ch 2, hdc2tog BLO, hdc BLO, hdc BLO to end, turn. (41 (43, 45, 47, 51) sts)

Row 18 (20, 23, 25, 26) (RS): Ch 2, hdc across until two sts rem, hdc2tog BLO, turn. (40 (42, 44, 46, 50) sts)

Rows 19–48 (21–52, 24–57, 26–61, 27–66): Rep Rows 17 and 18 (19 and 20, 22 and 23, 24 and 25, 25 and 26) 15 (16, 17, 18, 20) more times. (10 sts at end of row, 48 (52, 57, 61, 66) sts)

Rows 49–101 (53–105, 58–110, 62–114, 67–121): Ch 2, hdc BLO across. (10 sts)

Fasten off.

RIGHT COLLAR

Set-up Row: With RS facing, beg at center back of neck and working in opposite side of foundation ch, pull up loop in back loop of marked st, ch 2, hdc BLO across. (46 sts)

Rep Rows 1–48 (1–52, 1–57, 1–61, 1–66) of Left Collar.

Cont working ribbing while making buttonholes every 10th row:

Row 49 (53, 58, 62, 67): Ch 2, hdc BLO in next 3 sts, ch 2, skip next 2 sts, hdc BLO in last 5 sts, turn. (10 sts)

Rows 50–58 (54–62, 59–67, 63–71, 68–76): Ch 2, hdc BLO in each st, turn. (10 sts)

Rep Rows 49–58 (53–62, 58–67, 62–71, 67–76) 4 more times.

Rep Rows 49–51 (53–55, 58–60, 62–64, 67–71) once more.

Fasten off.

FINISHING

Using MC and yarn needle, sew Sleeves to Body at small gap in underarm. Using yarn tails and yarn needle, seam sleeves.

Weave in all ends.

ATTACHING COLLAR/BUTTON BAND

Crocheting along edges will add structure to front of sweater and make a tidy seam. Work edgings as foll:

SWEATER FRONT/NECK EDGING

Using D/3 (3.25mm) hook and MC, work 48 (48, 48, 48, 50) sc from bottom right corner to bottom of colorwork, 1 sc in 24 ch-1 sps along center front edge of colorwork ending at top, 44 (48, 50, 54, 58) sc along neck edge ending at side back corners of neck (at dec line), 30 (34, 40, 46, 50) sc across back neck, 44 (48, 50, 54, 58) sc along left neck edge ending at top of colorwork, 1 sc in 24 ch-1 sps along center front edge of colorwork ending at colorwork bottom, 48 (48, 48, 48, 50) sc along edge of left front ending at bottom corner.

Fasten off.

COLLAR/BUTTON BAND EDGING

Place collar/button placket on table so straight edge is toward you and left side of button placket (without buttonholes) is to right. Pull up loop of MC from marked corner ready to work across inc and dec edge of placket: 72 (72, 72, 72, 74) sc across edge of button placket ending at beg of collar shaping, 44 (48, 50, 54, 58) sc along shaped (diagonal) edge ending at corner where shaping ends, 30 (34, 40, 46, 50) sc across straight portion at back neck, 44 (48, 50, 54, 58) sc along next shaped (diagonal) edge ending at button placket, 72 (72, 72, 72, 74) sc along right button placket.

Using MC, sew Collar/Button Placket to front of sweater. Each edging has same number of sts so line up in 1:1 ratio.

Block sweater.

BUTTON REINFORCEMENTS

(make 6)

Round 1: Using E/4 (3.5mm) hook and MC, make an adjustable loop, 6 sc in loop, do not join but work in the round.

Round 2: 2 sc in each st, sl st to first sc to join.

Fasten off leaving long tail.

Sew each Button Reinforcement to WS of Left Button Band to line up with buttonholes. Using sewing needle and thread, sew buttons to RS of Left Button Band through button reinforcement. This creates a very durable button attachment.

Measurements

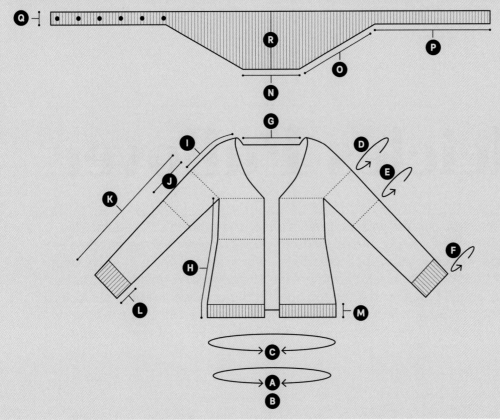

Badlands Cardigan	S	M	L	XL	2X
A. Chest (not including button Band)	32½in 82.5cm	37in 94cm	42in 106.5cm	45¾in 116cm	52in 132cm
B. Chest including button band	34½in 87.5cm	39in 99cm	44in 112cm	47¾in 21cm	54in 137cm
C. Hip (not including button band)	35in 89cm	39½in 100.5cm	44¾in 113.5cm	48¼in 121.5cm	54½in 138.5cm
D. Upper arm (at top of colorwork)	12in 30.5cm	13½in 34.5cm	15in 38cm	16½in 42cm	18¾in 47.5cm
E. Upper arm (at bottom of colorwork)	11in 28cm	12½in 32cm	14in 35.5cm	15in 38cm	17in 43cm
F. Wrist	9in 23cm	9¼in 23.5cm	10¼in 26cm	10¼in 26cm	11in 28cm
G. Across neck back	7½in 19cm	8½in 21.5cm	10½in 26.5cm	11¾in 30cm	12½in 32cm
H. Body length (from underarm to bottom edge of ribbing)	16¾in 42.5cm	16¾in 42.5cm	17in 43cm	17in 43cm	17½in 44.5cm
I. Shoulder length	7½in 19cm	8½in 21.5cm	9¼in 23.5cm	10½in 26.5cm	11¾in 30cm
J. Sleeve colorwork length	5¼in 13cm	5¼in 13cm	5¼in 13cm	5¼in 13cm	5¼in 13cm
K. Sleeve length	19in 48cm	19½in 49.5cm	19½in 49.5cm	20in 51cm	20in 51cm
L. Wrist ribbing length	2¾in 7cm	2¾in 7cm	2¾in 7cm	2¾in 7cm	2¾in 7cm
M. Hip ribbing length	1¾in 4.5cm	1¾in 4.5cm	1¾in 4.5cm	1¾in 4.5cm	1¾in 4.5cm
N. Collar back neck	7¾in 19.5cm	9in 23cm	10¾in 27.5cm	12in 30.5cm	12½in 32cm
O. Collar sides length	12in 33.5cm	13¼in 33.5cm	13¾in 35cm	14¾in 37.5cm	16½in 42cm
P. Button Band Length	16in 40.5cm	16in 40.5cm	16in 40.5cm	16in 40.5cm	16½in 42cm
Q. Button Band width (add ¼in [0.5cm] to width when button band is attached to front of sweater)	1¾in 4.5cm	1¾in 4.5cm	1¾in 4.5cm	1¾in 4.5cm	1¾in 4.5cm
R. Collar height at back neck	7¾in 19.5cm	8in 20cm	8¼in 21cm	8¾in 22cm	9½in 24cm

Icicles Pullover

This basic circular yoke pullover is easily customizable. The colorwork portion of the yoke is shaped by using decreasing hook sizes, so there are no decreases to interrupt the pattern—which means you can easily swap out this stitch pattern for another (see Swapping and Modifying Charts). The added bonus is that the top edge of the colorwork (at the neckline) is crocheted at a firm gauge, which helps it to keep its shape, whereas the bottom of the colorwork has lots of drape due to its looser gauge.

Finished size: XS, S, M, L, X, 2X, 3X; sized for 32 (35¾, 39, 42¾, 46¼, 50, 53¼)in/81 (91, 99, 108.5, 117.5, 127, 135)cm bust. Fit is close. Sample is shown in Medium worn with 3½in (9cm) of ease.

Note: The three largest sizes allow for a front chest measurement 2¼ (2¾, 3¼)in/ 5.75 (7, 8.25)cm larger than back chest to accommodate a larger bust.

Yarn: O Wool, O-Wash Sport, (100% Superwash Organic Merino; 304yd/278m per 3½oz/100g; CYCA #2); Devil's Pool, 5 (6, 6, 7, 7, 8, 8) hanks (MC); Barn Owl, 1 (1, 1, 1, 2, 2, 2) hank (CC).

Hook: Sizes E/4 (3.5mm), D/3 (3.25mm) and C/2 (2.75mm). Adjust hook size if necessary to obtain correct gauge.

Notions: Stitch markers; yarn needle.

Gauge (tension): 22 sts x 16 rounds = 4 x 4in (10 x 10cm) working ESC colorwork pattern using C/2 (2.75mm) hook.
17.5 sts x 15 rounds = 4 x 4in (10 x 10cm) working ESC in one color using D/3 (3.25mm) hook.
17.5 sts x 15 rounds = 4 x 4in (10 x 10cm) working ESC colorwork pattern using E/4 (3.5mm) hook.

Note: Once you have determined the hook size for the two colorwork gauges, use a hook between these two sizes for the mid-size hook.

Why I chose this yarn

This yarn is smooth and stretchy and has lots of drape—it is quite different from the yarn I chose for the Badlands Sweater because I wanted to show two contrasting examples for sweaters in the book. It is an organic superwash wool that is easy to care for and comes in such lovely colors!

Notes

This sweater has a surprising amount of stretch (up to 8–10% larger in width). However, the colorwork section does not stretch as much as the rest of the sweater.

Gauge note: if you determine your hook size for the smallest and largest hook used in colorwork, you can safely assume that a mid-size hook will be the hook size between the smallest and the largest. Use the mid-size hook to check gauge for the non-colorwork portion of the sweater. Most people crochet a bit tighter when working in colorwork, so it usually works to go down one hook size when switching from colorwork to one color in order to keep the gauge uniform. Everyone crochets a bit differently, however, so it is possible for the reverse to be true. Do not assume that your gauge will be the same when working in colorwork compared with working with only one color—for many people it is not.

When working ribbing, ch 2 tightly for the turning chain for a neater edge. You will not need to work into these ch sts so it doesn't matter if they are tight.

I prefer to attach ribbing onto an edge as I make it. This allows it to have maximum stretch (if you sew the ribbing on, the stretch will be restricted by your stitching). However, as you turn your work back and forth you will be turning the entire garment. This can be cumbersome, so I've developed a technique similar to turning the page in a book: After working across the RS of the ribbing and making slip stitches along the edge, hold the hook along the top edge, then turn the work and hook together (like turning a page backward). Now your work is facing the correct way for the next row, but your hook is pointing in the wrong direction. Bring the yarn tail under the hook and around the edge of the work to the back, then continue to rotate just the

hook in a counter-clockwise direction 180 degrees (as viewed from the top) until it is pointing the correct way.

Decrease charts: To keep colorwork looking even, the decreases at the top of the yoke are in different places for each size. Make sure you are using the correct chart, and do not forget to finish the yoke section after working through the chart (most sizes have additional rounds that are not charted because they are a solid color). The plain gray boxes are a placeholder; they do not represent a stitch. The gray box with the diagonal line represents the first leg of an ESC2tog stitch so when you get to one make an ESC2tog decrease over the next 2 sts. Always make decrease stitches using MC.

Blocking notes: Be sure to block your sweater when finished. This will even out decreases in the yoke, enhance the colorwork, and smooth the transition from yoke to body. When this sweater gets wet, it is prone to stretching lengthwise. Take the time to shape it to the correct measurements before letting it dry. This is a small price to pay for having a very stretchy sweater with loads of drape (aka: super flattering sweater)!

Stitch guide

ESC (extended single crochet): Insert hook in next st, yo and pull up a loop, yo and pull through just one loop, yo and pull through two loops.

ModESC2tog (extended single crochet 2 stitches together modified): This is worked over the next two stitches, and decreases your stitch count by one stitch. Insert hook under just front loop of next st, then insert hook under both loops of foll st (from front to back, as normal), yo and pull up a loop, yo and pull through just one loop, yo and pull through two loops.

Icicles yoke chart all sizes

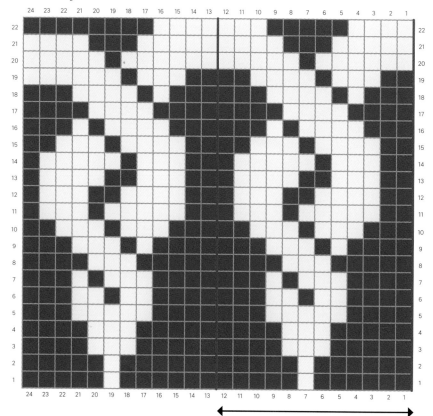

Work section between red lines
17 (19, 21, 23, 25, 27, 29) times.

PULLOVER PATTERN

YOKE

Worked from the bottom up. Using E/4 (3.5mm) hook and MC, ch 217 (241, 265, 289, 313, 337, 361).

Set-up row: Beg in 2nd ch from hook and working in bottom of ch, ESC in each ch across. (216 (240, 264, 288, 312, 336, 360) sts)

PM in first st. Beg with marked st to work in the round without joins, ESC in each st around, working Rounds 1–11 of Icicles Yoke Chart. 18 (20, 22, 24, 26, 28) icicles around)

Change to D/3 (3.25mm) hook and work Rounds 12–17 of Icicles Yoke Chart.

Change to C/2 (2.75mm) hook and work Rounds 18–22 of Icicles Yoke Chart.

YOKE DECREASES

Note: For stability and gauge consistency, continue to work over non-working color on rounds that do not require color changes.

FOR SIZE XS ONLY

Beg working from Icicles Decrease Chart Size X-Small.

Round 1: [ESC in next 4 sts, ESC2tog, ESC in next 6 sts] 20 times. (198 sts)

Round 2: ESC around.

Round 3: [ESC in next 8 sts, ESC2tog, ESC in next st] 20 times. (180 sts)

Rounds 4 and 5: ESC around.

Round 6: Using MC and cont to work over CC for extra stability, [ESC in next 16 sts, ESC2tog] 10 times. (170 sts)

Cut CC yarn. Do not fasten off, cont to Neck Ribbing.

FOR SIZE S ONLY

Beg working from Icicles Decrease Chart Size Small.

Round 1: [ESC in next 4 sts, ESC2tog, ESC in next 5 sts] 21 times. (221 sts)

Round 2: ESC around.

Round 3: [ESC in next 8 sts, ESC2tog, ESC in next st] 21 times. (200 sts)

Round 4: ESC around.

Round 5: [ESC in next 2 sts, ESC2tog, ESC in next 7 sts] 21 times. (180 sts)

Round 6: Using MC and cont to work over CC for extra stability, [ESC in next 16 sts, ESC2tog] 10 times. (170 sts)

Cut CC yarn. Do not fasten off, cont to Neck Ribbing.

FOR SIZE M ONLY

Beg working from Icicles Decrease Chart Size M.

Round 1: [ESC in next 4 sts, ESC2tog, ESC in next 6 sts] 22 times. (242 sts)

Round 2: ESC around.

Round 3: [ESC in next 8 sts, ESC2tog, ESC in next st] 22 times. (220 sts)

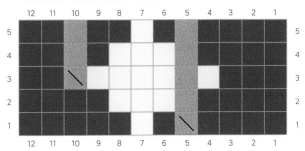

Icicles decrease chart size XS

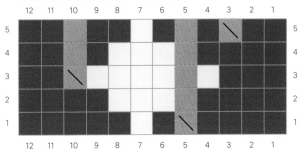

Icicles decrease chart size S

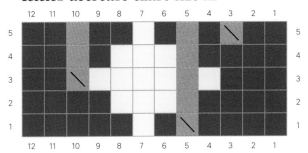

Icicles decrease chart size M

Round 4: ESC around.

Round 5: [ESC in next 2 sts, ESC2tog, ESC in next 6 sts] 22 times. (198 sts)

Round 6: Using MC and cont to work over CC for extra stability, ESC around.

Round 7: [ESC in next 7 sts, ESC2tog] 22 times. (176 sts)

Round 8: ESC around. (176 sts)

Cut CC yarn. Do not fasten off, cont to Neck Ribbing.

FOR SIZE L ONLY

Beg working from Icicles Decrease Chart Size L.

Round 1: [ESC in next 4 sts, ESC2tog, ESC in next 6 sts] 24 times. (264 sts)

Rounds 2 and 3: ESC around.

Round 4: [ESC in next 7 sts, ESC2tog, ESC in next 2 sts] 24 times. (240 sts)

Rounds 5 and 6: ESC around.

Round 7: [ESC in next st, ESC2tog, ESC in next 7 sts] 24 times. (216 sts)

Round 8: Using MC and cont to work over CC for extra stability, ESC around.

Round 9: [ESC in next 7 sts, ESC2tog] 24 times. (192 sts)

Round 10: ESC around.

Round 11: [ESC in next 14 sts, ESC2tog] 12 times. (180 sts)

Cut CC yarn. Do not fasten off, cont to Neck Ribbing.

FOR SIZE XL ONLY

Beg working from Icicles Decrease Chart Size XL.

Round 1: [ESC in next 4 sts, ESC2tog, ESC in next 6 sts] 26 times. (286 sts)

Rounds 2–4: ESC around.

Round 5: [ESC in next 8 sts, ESC2tog, ESC in next st] 26 times. (260 sts)

Rounds 6 and 7: ESC around.

Round 8: This round dec Yoke at front more than back. Using MC and cont to work over CC for extra stability throughout rem of Yoke, [ESC in next 4 sts, ESC2tog, ESC in next 10 sts, ESC2tog, ESC in next 5 sts] 5 times, [ESC in next 3 sts, ESC2tog, ESC in next 4 sts] 15 times (PM in bottom of yoke directly below point of icicle nearest center of 8th rep), ESC in next 4 sts, ESC2tog, ESC in next 4 sts. (234 sts)

Marker indicates center front of Yoke. Use this later to determine center back of Yoke when directed to do so.

Rounds 9–11: ESC around (234 sts)

Round 12: This round dec Yoke at front more than back. [ESC in next st, ESC2tog, ESC in next 9 sts, ESC2tog, ESC in next 7 sts] 5 times, [ESC in next st, ESC2tog, ESC in next 5 sts] 15 times, ESC in next st, ESC2tog, ESC in next 6 sts. (208 sts)

Rounds 13–14: ESC around

Round 15: [ESC in next 6 sts, ESC2tog] 8 times. (182 sts)

Round 16: ESC around.

Cut CC yarn. Do not fasten off, cont to Neck Ribbing.

FOR SIZE 2X ONLY

Beg working from Icicles Decrease Chart Size 2X.

Round 1: [ESC in next 4 sts, ESC2tog, ESC in next 6 sts] 28 times. (308 sts)

Rounds 2–4: ESC around.

Round 5: [ESC in next 9 sts, ESC2tog] 28 times. (280 sts)

Rounds 6 and 7: ESC around.

Round 8: Using MC and cont to work over CC for extra stability throughout rem of Yoke, ESC around.

Round 9: This round dec Yoke at front more than back) [ESC in next 5 sts, ESC2tog, ESC in next 5 sts] 10 times, 1 ESC in next 2 sts, [ESC in next 3 sts, ESC2tog, ESC in next 7 sts, ESC2tog, ESC in next 3 sts] 8 times (PM in bottom of yoke directly below point of icicle nearest beg of 5th rep), ESC in next 3 sts, ESC2tog, ESC in next 10 sts, ESC2tog, ESC in next 5 sts. (252 sts)

Marker indicates center front of Yoke. Use this later to determine center back of Yoke when directed to do so.

Rounds 10–12: ESC around. (252 sts)

Round 13: [Esc in next 7 sts, ESC2tog] 28 times. (224 sts)

Rounds 14–16: ESC around.

Round 17: This round dec Yoke at front more than back. [ESC in next 4 sts, ESC2tog, ESC in next 4 sts] 10 times, ESC in next st, [ESC in next 3 sts, ESC2tog, ESC in next 2 sts, ESC in next 2 sts, ESC2tog, ESC in next 2 sts] 8 times, ESC in next 3 sts, ESC2tog, ESC in next 3 sts. (196 sts.)

Rounds 18–19: ESC around.

Round 20: [Esc in next 2 sts, ESC2tog] 14 times. (182 sts)

Cut CC yarn. Do not fasten off, cont to Neck Ribbing.

Icicles decrease chart size L

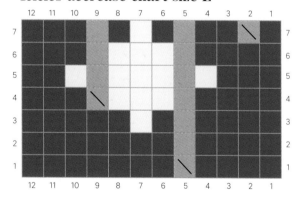

Icicles decrease chart size XL

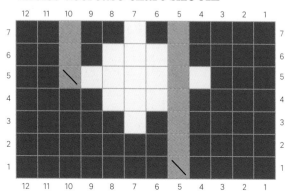

Icicles decrease chart size 2X

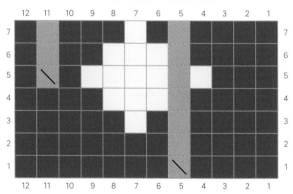

Icicles decrease chart size 3X

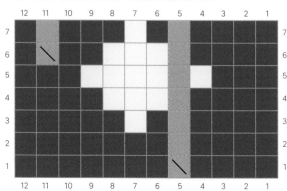

FOR SIZE 3X ONLY

Beg working from Icicles Decrease Chart Size 3X.

Round 1: [ESC in next 4 sts, ESC2tog, ESC in next 6 sts] 30 times. (330 sts)

Rounds 2–5: ESC around.

Round 6: [ESC in next 9 sts, ESC2tog] 30 times. (300 sts)

Round 7: ESC around.

Rounds 8–10: Using MC and cont to work over CC for extra stability throughout remainder of Yoke, ESC around.

Round 11: This round dec Yoke at front of sweater more than back. [ESC in next 5 sts, ESC2tog, ESC in next 5 sts] 11 times, ESC in next 2 sts, [ESC in next 3 sts, ESC2tog, ESC in next 7 sts, ESC2tog, ESC in next 3 sts] 9 times (PM in bottom of Yoke directly below point of icicle nearest center of 5th rep), ESC in next 6 sts, ESC2tog, ESC in next 5 sts. (270 sts)

Marker indicates center front of Yoke. Use this later to determine center back of Yoke when directed to do so.

Rounds 12–15: ESC around.

Round 16: [ESC in next 7 sts, ESC2tog] 30 times. (240 sts)

Rounds 17–20: ESC around.

Round 21: This round dec Yoke at front more than back. [ESC in next 3 sts, ESC2tog, ESC in next 8 sts, ESC2tog, ESC next 4 sts] 5 times, ESC in next 4 sts, ESC2tog, ESC in next 8 sts [ESC in next 2 sts, ESC2tog, ESC in next 5 sts, ESC2tog, ESC in next 2 sts] 9 times, ESC in next 7 sts, ESC2tog, ESC in next 5 sts. (210 sts)

Rounds 22–23: ESC around.

Round 24: [ESC in next 8 sts, ESC2tog] 20 times, ESC in next 10 sts. (190 sts)

Cut CC yarn. Do not fasten off, cont to Neck Ribbing.

NECK RIBBING

Make ribbing at same time as working sl sts around neck opening as foll:

Row 1: Ch 10, beg in 3rd ch from hook, and working in bottom of ch, 1 hdc in each ch across. (8 sts)

Row 2: Sl st in next 3 sts of neck opening (sl sts do not count as sts), rotate to work 1 hdc BLO in each hdc of ribbing as foll: insert hook in 2nd to last sl st along neck edge, yo and pull up a loop, insert hook under back loop of last hdc made, yo and pull up a loop, yo and pull through all 3 loops on hook (first hdc BLO made—this method reduces appearance of holes

between ribbing and neck edge), hdc BLO in next 7 hdc. (8 sts)

Row 3: Ch 2, turn, hdc BLO across ribbing. (8 sts)

Row 4: Sl st in next 4 sts of neck opening (sl sts do not count as sts), rotate to work 1 hdc BLO in each hdc of ribbing as foll: insert hook in 2nd to last sl st along neck edge, yo and pull up a loop, insert hook under back loop of last hdc made, yo and pull up a loop, yo and pull through all 3 loops on hook (first hdc BLO made), hdc BLO in next 7 hdc. (8 sts)

Row 5: Ch 2, turn, hdc BLO across ribbing. (8 sts)

Rep Rows 2–5 around neck opening—there are 2 (2, 1, 5, 0, 0, 0) sts at neck opening left.

Note: For sizes XL (2XL, 3XL) end after working a rep of Row 4—DO NOT work last rep of Row 5.

FOR SIZE L ONLY

Rep Rows 2–3 once more.

FOR SIZES XS (S, M, L) ONLY

Sl st in next 2 (2, 1, 2) sts of neck opening (sl sts do not count as sts), rotate to work 1 hdc BLO in each hdc of ribbing as foll: insert hook in second to last sl st along neck edge, yo and pull up a loop, insert hook under back loop of last hdc made, yo and pull up a loop, yo and pull through all 3 loops on hook, hdc BLO in next 7 hdc. (8 sts)

FOR ALL SIZES

Seaming row: Ch 1, turn, place foundation row behind last row worked. Sl st edges together working through both loops of last row worked and BLO of foundation ch. (8 sl sts across)

Fasten off.

SHORT ROW SHAPING (AT BOTTOM OF YOKE)

Notes: All short rows are worked with RS facing. Fasten off when directed.

To reduce the number of yarn tails to be woven in, crochet over them on the next round. This can even be done toward the end of the short row by bringing the previous row's tail forward to crochet over it.

PM at bottom of Yoke to mark center back—beg rounds (of Yoke) and sl st seam on ribbed neckline should be somewhere on back of work (I prefer them to be on back of one shoulder and not near center back). Tip of an icicle should be directly at

center back (PM in st directly below Icicle tip). If making size XL (2X, 3X) you will have already marked center front, so find icicle point directly opposite front point.

Hold yoke upside down so that foundation edge is ready to be worked into. Change to D/3 (3.25mm) hook.

Short Row 1: Counting backwards from marker, pull up loop of MC in 9th (10th, 12th, 15th, 17th, 19th, 22nd) st before marker, ch 1 (does not count as a st here and throughout), beg with same marked st, ESC in next 19 (21, 25, 31, 35, 39, 45) sts.

Fasten off. Leave marker at center back of Yoke to ensure short rows are worked evenly.

Short Row 2: Counting backwards from first st of Short Row 1, pull up loop in 13th (13th, 14th, 14th, 15th, 16th, 17th) st, ch 1, beg with same st, ESC in next 13 (13, 14, 14, 15, 16, 17) sts, ESC in next 19 (21, 25, 31, 35, 39, 45) sts of previous short row, Esc in next 13 (13, 14, 14, 15, 16, 17) sts.

Fasten off.

Short Row 3: Counting backwards from first st of Short Row 2, pull up loop in 13th (13th, 14th, 14th, 15th, 16th, 17th) st, ch 1, beg with same st, ESC in next 13 (13, 14, 14, 15, 16, 17) sts, ESC in next 45 (47, 53, 59, 65, 71, 79) sts of previous short row, ESC in next 13 (13, 14, 14, 15, 16, 17) sts.

Fasten off.

Short Row 4: Counting backwards from first st of Short Row 3, pull up loop in 13th (13th, 14th, 14th, 15th, 16th, 17th) st, ch 1, beg with same st, ESC in next 13 (13, 14, 14, 15, 16, 17) sts, ESC in next 71 (73, 81, 87, 95, 103, 113) sts of previous short row, ESC in next 13 (13, 14, 14, 15, 16, 17) sts.

Fasten off.

Short Row 5: Counting backwards from first st of Short Row 4, pull up loop in 13th (13th, 14th, 14th, 15th, 16th, 17th) st, ch 1, beg with same st, ESC in next 13 (13, 14, 14, 15, 16, 17) sts, ESC in next 97 (99, 109, 115, 125, 135, 147) sts of previous short row, ESC in next 13 (13, 14, 14, 15, 16, 17) sts. (123 (125, 137, 143, 155, 167, 181) sts in short row)

PM in 30th (27th, 29th, 29th, 33rd, 36th, 40th) st of this short row. Fasten off.

Beg with marked st, pull up a loop, ch 1, 65 (73, 81, 87, 91, 97, 103) ESC across back, ch 4 (4, 4, 5, 5, 6, 6) at underarm, skip next 42 (46, 51, 56, 60, 65, 70) sts for Sleeve, 67 (75, 81, 89, 101, 109, 117) ESC across front, ch 4, skip next 42 (46, 51, 56, 60, 65, 70) sts for Sleeve, do not join but cont to work in rounds beg with first st of this round. PM to keep track of beg of rounds.

Work 48 (48, 48, 50, 50, 52, 54) rounds until body measures 12½ (12½, 12½, 13, 13, 13½, 14)in/32 (32, 32, 33, 33, 34.5, 35.5) cm from underarm to waist edge. Do not fasten off.

Note: Ribbing will add another 2in (5cm) to body length, and blocking will add length along side seam areas (see note about blocking).

RIBBING

Make ribbing at same time as working sl sts around bottom edge of sweater as foll:

Row 1: Ch 16, beg in 3rd ch from hook, and working in bottom of ch, hdc in each ch across. (14 sts)

Row 2: Sl st in next 2 sts of bottom edge (sl sts do not count as sts), rotate to work 1 hdc BLO in next 14 hdc. (14 sts)

Row 3: Ch 2, turn, hdc BLO across ribbing. (14 sts)

Rep Rows 2 and 3 around bottom edge until 2 sts left.

Rep Row 2 once more.

Seaming row: Ch 1, turn, place foundation row behind last row worked, sl st edges together working through both loops of last row worked and BLO of foundation ch. (14 sl sts across)

Fasten off.

SLEEVES

Round 1: Pull up a loop in bottom of ch sts at center of underarm 2 (2, 2, 2, 2, 3, 3) sts before marked st, ch 1 (does not count as a st), ESC in next 2 (2, 2, 2, 2, 3, 3) sts at underarm, ESC in place where body meets Sleeve, ESC in marked st and foll 41 (45, 50, 55, 59, 64, 69) sts of arm, 1 ESC in place where body meets Sleeve, 1 ESC st in bottom of each rem 2 (2, 2, 3, 3, 3, 3) ch sts ending at center of underarm, do not join but work in round, PM in beg of round. (48 (52, 57, 63, 67, 73, 78) sts around arm)

FOR SIZE XS ONLY

Rounds 2–8: ESC around.

Round 9: ModESC2tog, ESC around until 2 sts rem, ModESC2tog. (46 sts)

Rounds 10–26: ESC around.

Rep Rounds 9–26. (44 sts)

Rep Rounds 9–22. (42 sts)

Do not fasten off.

FOR SIZE S ONLY

Rounds 2–8: ESC around.

Round 9: ModESC2tog, ESC around until 2 sts rem, ModESC2tog. (50 sts)

Rounds 10–18: ESC around.

Rep Rounds 10–18 four more times. (42 sts at end).

Do not fasten off.

FOR SIZE M ONLY

Rounds 2–8: ESC around.

Round 9: ModESC2tog, ESC around until 2 sts rem, ModESC2tog. (55 sts)

Rounds 10–18: ESC around.

Rep Rounds 9–18 four more times. (47 sts at end).

Rep Rounds 9–11. (45 sts)

Do not fasten off.

FOR SIZE L ONLY

Rounds 2–4: ESC around.

Round 5: ModESC2tog, ESC around until 2 sts rem, ModESC2tog. (61 sts)

Rounds 6–10: ESC around.

Rep Rounds 5–10 eight more times. (45 sts at end)

Do not fasten off.

FOR SIZE XL ONLY

Rounds 2–3: ESC around.

Round 4: ModESC2tog, ESC around until 2 sts rem, ModESC2tog. (65 sts)

Rounds 5–9: ESC around.

Rep Rounds 4–9 eight more times. (49 sts at end)

Rep Rounds 4–6. (47 sts)

Do not fasten off.

FOR SIZE 2X ONLY

Rounds 2–6: ESC around.

Round 7: ModESC2tog, ESC around until 2 sts rem, ModESC2tog. (71 sts)

Rounds 8–10: ESC around.

Rep Rounds 7–10 twelve more times. (47 sts at end)

Do not fasten off.

FOR SIZE 3X ONLY

Round 2: ESC around.

Round 3: ModESC2tog, ESC around until 2 sts rem, ModESC2tog. (76 sts)

Rounds 4–6: ESC around.

Rep Rounds 3–6 thirteen more times. (50 sts at end)

Do not fasten off.

CUFF

Make ribbing for cuff at same time as working sl sts around bottom edge of sleeve as foll:

Row 1: Ch 22, beg with 3rd ch from hook, and working in bottom of ch, hdc in each ch across. (20 sts)

Row 2: Sl st in next 2 sts of wrist opening (sl sts do not count as sts), rotate to work 1 hdc BLO in next 20 hdc. (20 sts)

Row 3: Ch 2, turn, hdc BLO across ribbing. (20 sts)

Rep Rows 2 and 3 around sleeve opening until there is 1 st left.

Sl st in last st of wrist opening, rotate to work 1 hdc BLO in next 20 hdc. (20 sts)

Seaming row: Ch 1, turn, place foundation row behind last row worked, sl st edges together working through both loops of last row worked and BLO of foundation ch. (29 sl sts across)

Fasten off.

FINISHING

Sew any holes closed at underarm using yarn tails. Weave in loose ends. Block (see Notes).

Measurements

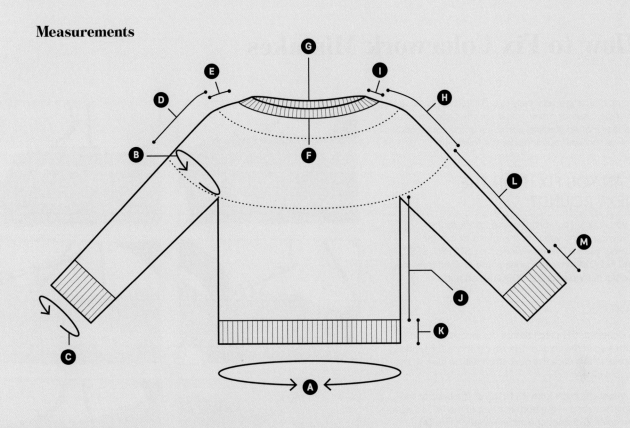

Icicles Pullover	XS	S	M	L	XL	2X	3X
A. Chest	32in 81cm	35¾in 91cm	39in 99cm	42¾in 108.5cm	46¼in 117.5cm	50in 127cm	53¼in 135cm
B. Upper sleeve circumference	11in 28cm	12in 30.5cm	13in 33cm	14½in 37cm	15¼in 39cm	16¾in 42.5cm	18in 45.5cm
C. Wrist circumference	9½in 24cm	9¾in 24.5cm	10¼in 26cm	10¼in 26cm	10¾in 27.5cm	10¾in 27.5cm	11½in 29cm
D. Yoke colorwork length	6¼in 16cm	6¼in 16cm	6¼in 16cm	6¼in 16cm	6¼in 16cm	6¼in 16cm	6¼in 16cm
E. Length above colorwork (before ribbing)	1½in 4cm	1½in 4cm	1¾in 4.5cm	2½in 6.5cm	3½in 9cm	4½in 11.5cm	5¼in 13.5cm
F. Neck opening (circumference) before ribbing is added	31in 78.5cm	30¾in 78cm	32in 81cm	32½in 82.5cm	33in 84cm	33in 84cm	34½in 87.5cm
G. Neck opening (circumference) after ribbing is added	25in 63.5cm	25in 63.5cm	26in 66cm	26½in 67.5cm	26¾in 68cm	26¾in 68cm	28in 71cm
H. Total yoke length	7¾in 19.5cm	7¾in 19.5cm	8in 20cm	8¾in 202cm	9¾in 24.5cm	10¾in 27.5cm	11½in 29cm
I. Ribbing width at neck	1¼in 3cm	1¼in 3cm	1¼in 3cm	1¼in 3cm	1¼in 3cm	1¼in 3cm	1¼in 3cm
J. Body length before blocking	12½in 32cm	12½in 32cm	12½in 32cm	13in 33cm	13in 33cm	13½in 35cm	14in 35.5cm
J. Body length after blocking	13in 33cm	13in 33cm	13in 33cm	13½in 34cm	13½in 34cm	14in 35.5cm	14½in 35.5cm
K. Ribbing width at hip	2in 5cm	2in 5cm	2in 5cm	2in 5cm	2in 5cm	2in 5cm	2in 5cm
L. Sleeve length	15in 38cm	15in 38cm	15½in 39.5cm	15in 38cm	15½in 39.5cm	15in 38cm	14½in 37cm
M. Cuff width	3in 7.5cm	3in 7.5cm	3in 7.5cm	3in 7.5cm	3in 7.5cm	3in 7.5cm	3in 7.5cm

How to Fix Colorwork Mistakes

Some charts are very easy to work without making a mistake... but for many, this is not the case. So what happens when you find a mistake in the colorwork? Before you rip it out consider the following:

CAN YOU FIX IT ON THE NEXT ROUND?

If you realize your mistake when working the following round you may be able to fix it in the current round. This only works for CSC, ESC, SESC, and FPDC stitches (because of the unused front loop, it does not work for the SCBLO stitch pattern).

FOR CSC

1. Complete the stitch before the incorrect stitch with a yo in the color of the next stitch in the working round. In this case the next stitch will be blue so the yo is in blue.

2. Insert the hook from RS to WS at the base of the incorrect stitch—the bottom point of the "V". Yo with the color to change the incorrect stitch into **(A)**.

3. Pull up a loop. Insert the hook between the legs of the incorrect stitch (as to begin a normal CSC st), yo with the color that the next stitch will be **(B)**.

4. Pull a loop through the incorrect stitch and through the next loop on the hook. Yo with the color of the working round stitch **(C)**.

5. Pull through both loops: the incorrect stitch is fixed, and the next CSC stitch in the round is complete **(D)**.

FOR ESC

6. Complete the stitch before the incorrect stitch with a yo in the color of the next stitch in the working round. In this case, the next stitch will be blue, so the yo is in blue.

7. Insert the hook from RS to WS at the base of the incorrect stitch, where the arrow is pointing **(E)**, at the bottom point of the lower "V" shape.

8. Yo with the color to change the incorrect stitch into **(F)** and pull up loop. Insert the hook in the top of the same incorrect stitch, between the top two legs (like making a normal SESC stitch), yo with same color **(G)** and pull up loop, then pull through one loop on the hook (2 loops on hook) **(H)**.

9. Insert the hook in the incorrect stitch, under both top loops (like beginning an ESC st), yo with the color of the next working round stitch (in this case blue) **(I)**.

10. Pull a loop through the incorrect stitch and through the next loop on the hook. Yo with the same color **(J)** and pull through one loop.

11. Yo with the same color, and pull through both loops: the incorrect stitch is fixed, and the next ESC stitch in the working round is complete **(K)**.

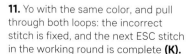

FOR SESC

12. Complete the stitch before the incorrect stitch with a yo in the color of the next stitch in the working round. In this case, the next stitch will be white so the yo is in white.

13. Insert the hook from RS to WS at the base of the incorrect stitch, the bottom point of the lower "V" shape. Yo with the color to change the incorrect stitch into (in this case, blue) **(H)**.

14. Pull up a loop. Insert the hook in the top of the same incorrect stitch, between the top two legs, (like making a normal SESC) stitch, yo with the same color **(I)** and pull up a loop, pull through one loop on the hook (2 loops on hook).

15. Insert the hook in the incorrect stitch, under both top loops (like a normal ESC st), yo with the color of the next working round stitch (in this case white) **(J)**.

16. Pull a loop through the incorrect stitch and through the next loop on the hook, yo with the same color and pull through one loop.

17. Yo with the same color, and pull through both loops: the incorrect stitch is fixed, and the next SESC stitch in the working round is complete **(K)**.

FOR FPDC

18. Complete the stitch before the incorrect stitch with a yo in the color of the next stitch in the working round. In this case the next stitch will be blue so the yo is in blue.

19. The replacement post stitch needs to be anchored around the same post as the incorrect stitch. The arrow shows where the hook will be inserted **(L)**.

20. Yo with the color to change the incorrect stitch into, insert the hook from front to back to front, and from right to left (for lefties: from front to back to front and from left to right) around the post of the stitch below the incorrect stitch. Yo with the replacement stitch color **(M)**.

21. Bring the loop back through (around the back of the post to the front), yo with the same color, pull through two loops. Yo with the color of the next working round stitch **(N)** and pull through one loop.

22. Yo with the same color. Insert the hook around the post of the incorrect stitch and the post of the new stitch, as shown by the arrow **(O)**. Yo with the same color, trapping the old color **(P)**.

23. Bring the loop around the back of the post, to the front, yo with the same color, and pull through two loops. Yo with same color and pull through the last three loops: the incorrect stitch is fixed, and the next FPDC stitch in the working round is complete **(Q)**.

DUPLICATE STITCHES

If you made the mistake a few rounds below, or if you prefer to fix your mistake later, you can add a duplicate stitch on top of the incorrect stitch at any time. This does not work well for the SCBLO stitch pattern (because of that unused front loop), but for the other stitch patterns the duplicate stitch is a great choice—it blends in well and is easy to do, you just have to remember to do it. It may help to mark problems with stitch markers so that you don't need to search for them later.

FOR CSC DUPLICATE

This is just like making a duplicate stitch in knitting, using a yarn needle and yarn of the correct color.

1. Bring the needle from WS to RS at the bottom of the "V" of the incorrect stitch, then under both legs of the stitch above from right to left (for lefties: from left to right) **(A)**.

2. Insert the needle back through the bottom of the incorrect stitch from RS to WS **(B)**. Weave in the ends. You will not even be able to see your mistake **(C)**!

FOR ESC DUPLICATE

This is very similar to making a CSC duplicate stitch— the only difference is that you are making two "V" shapes, one stacked right on top of the other for each incorrect stitch.

1. Using a yarn needle and yarn of the correct color, bring the needle from WS to RS at the bottom of the top "V" of the incorrect stitch, then slide the needle under the vertical bar just above the top "V" from right to left (For lefties: from left to right) **(D)**.

2. Insert the needle back through the bottom of the incorrect stitch from RS to WS **(E)**.

3. Next, bring the needle from WS to RS at the bottom of the lower "V" of the incorrect stitch, then slide it behind both legs of the duplicate top "V" **(F)**.

4. Take needle back to the WS at the bottom of the stitch to complete the second (bottom) half of the duplicate stitch. Now the incorrect stitch has been fixed **(G)**.

FOR SESC DUPLICATE

Again you are making two "V" shapes, one stacked right on top of the other for each incorrect stitch.

1. Using a yarn needle and yarn of the correct color, bring the needle from WS to RS at the bottom of the top "V" of the incorrect stitch, then slide the needle under the vertical bar just above from right to left (for lefties: from left to right) **(H)**.

2. Insert the needle back through the bottom of the incorrect stitch from RS to WS **(I)**.

3. Bring the needle from WS to RS at the bottom point of the lower "V" of the incorrect stitch, then slide your needle behind both legs of the duplicate top "V" **(J)**.

4. Take the needle back to the WS at the bottom of the stitch to complete the second (bottom) half of the duplicate stitch. Now the incorrect stitch has been fixed **(K)**!

FOR FPDC DUPLICATE

For this stitch, use a crochet hook and yarn of the correct color to make a post stitch on top of the incorrect post stitch.

1. Insert the hook under the horizontal strands (from bottom to top) in the groove just before the incorrect stitch (the groove between stitches), yo **(L)**, and pull up a loop, ch 1 **(M)**.

2. Yo, insert the hook around the post of the stitch just below the incorrect stitch (as for a normal FPDC), and complete a normal FPDC as follows: yo **(N)**.

3. Bring a loop around the back of the post to the front, yo **(O)** and pull through two loops, yo and pull through two loops **(P)**. Fasten off.

4. Use the yarn tails to secure the top and left side of the new post stitch to the fabric behind it. Weave in ends. The stitch has been corrected **(Q)**.

Swapping and Modifying Charts

We all want to make things to our own liking—that's why we are crocheters! This section will help you change a chart to fit your preferences, so that you can make it your own way!

STRAIGHT-UP SWAPPING

Swapping one colorwork chart for another of the same size is an easy way to customize your project. Simply replace the current chart with the new chart—this works if the charts have the same number of stitches and rows, and with projects that don't have an obvious Center Front line, like the Snowy Picture Hat.

If you are making a project that has a center front line (like the Icicles Pullover), you will need to check one additional thing: if there is an obvious visual center of the current chart either vertically, or horizontally, you should match the new chart center up with that line of the chart. For example, in the Icicles Yoke Chart, the repeating motif has a visual center on the seventh stitch. The replacement chart will need the visual center of the repeating motif in the same place, or it may look off center in the sweater yoke. Take a look at the chart for Waves of Grain (see The Swatches: ESC Swatches). This chart has the same number of stitches and rounds, AND the visual center of the motif is on stitch 7 as well, so it would be an easy exchange.

If your new chart does not have a visual center, like Great Divide (see Swatch Charts: CSC Swatches), then this is not a concern. If your chart does have a visual center, but it's not in the same place, you can rearrange the columns or rounds until the visual center lines up in the right place: Make a copy of the chart, highlight the visual center, then move columns or rows from one side of the chart to the other until the visual center is where you want it to be (see the Narwhal School example **(C)**).

MODIFYING A CHART TO FIT

So what happens if the chart that you want to use isn't an exact match for stitches or rows? Here are some ways to alter your chart in order to make it fit:

THE CHART IS SMALLER THAN THE ORIGINAL

Let's say you are making the Claddagh Mittens, but you want to substitute with a piece of the Narwhal School chart. The charted area from one single narwhal has fewer stitches and rows and the visual center is not in the same place as the Claddagh Upper Chart **(A, B)**. You could use the bottom 13 rounds of the Narwhal School chart, and then add one column of stitches in MC along the side to achieve the correct number of stitches. To correct the round count, we can add some extra rounds of MC to make it the same as the Upper Claddagh chart. The Narwhal still looks off-center, so I removed one column of stitches from the left and added it to the right side. Then when we add in the chart details from the four bottom rounds of the Claddagh Upper Chart we can see what is leftover to fill in with MC **(C)**.

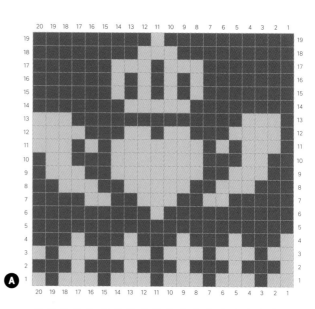

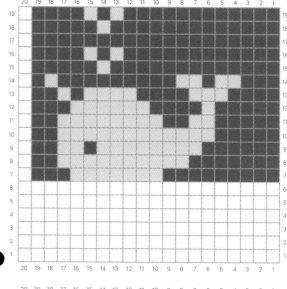

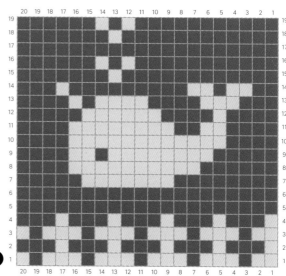

THE CHART IS BIGGER THAN THE ORIGINAL

If the pattern has a repeating chart, figure out the total number of stitches around (in your size) and use that number as the end-goal. For example, if you are working a hat that uses a chart of 20 sts, and the chart repeats five times around the hat, you have 100 stitches around to work with. This means that you can use a chart with any multiple of 100. You could repeat a 10-stitch chart 10 times (10 x 10 = 100), a 25-stitch chart four times or a 50-stitch chart twice, and so on. But what if you want to use a 22-stitch chart? You have a few options:

1. The 22-stitch chart worked five times gives ten more stitches than the pattern calls for. You could try swatching with a smaller hook to see if you could just make the hat with ten extra stitches. If this works, you will not need to modify the chart, but you will need to modify the rest of the pattern. For something simple like a hat it may not be a problem, but for a more involved project it might require some patterning know-how. If your stitch count is only off by a few stitches or rounds, you might get away with a slightly different count. Check if this would change the size of what you are making, or could you make up for the difference elsewhere?

2. You could modify the chart by removing two columns of stitches. Depending on your stitch pattern, this may or may not be noticeable.

3. You could ADD three columns of stitches to the chart and then work one fewer repeat around (22 + 3) x 4 = 100.

4. You could repeat the chart four times, and then add a 12-stitch chart element as an accent.

Note: The ideas above hold true for modifying the round count as well.

PROJECT SUBSTITUTIONS

If you are interested in swapping out the charts for the projects in this book, please see the hints and guidelines below.

BADLANDS CARDIGAN

Swapping out the chart for this cardigan can be an easy process for certain types of images, but for other colorwork charts it will require a bit more effort. In this section we will explore both of these scenarios, so that you have the confidence to tailor the charts to your needs.

EASY SWAPS FOR BADLANDS CARDIGAN

Use a pattern that doesn't need to have full repeats to look good— such as the Great Divide (see The Swatches: CSC Swatches) omitting rounds 1 and 26 of the chart, Single Crochet! or Spatter (see The Swatches: CSC Swatches), or Forest (see The Swatches: ESC Swatches. Begin with an MC set-up Round, and repeat the chart as needed.

Note: This only works in this piece because there is an opening down the center front of the cardigan so the image does not need to connect beginning-to-end. This connection does happen under the sleeves, but it is well hidden so should not be a visual problem.

Things to look for in a chart that doesn't need to have full repeats:

1. A chart that is asymmetrical, and appears to be organic or random in design.

2. A chart that is wide enough so that it doesn't have obvious repeats in it.

3. A chart that has very small repeats (such as Checks: see The Swatches: FPDC Swatches) so that it won't be obvious if the fronts of your cardigan do not match or mirror.

SWAPPING CHARTS WITH A BIT MORE THOUGHT

To substitute a colorwork chart in the Badlands Cardigan, it's important to know how many stitches there are across the colorwork sections. For the Body at the chest there are 125 (143, 163, 177, 201) sts. For the Sleeves there are 46 (52, 58, 64, 72) sts at the widest (top) edge. The colorwork sections are 24 rounds tall, including the MC set-up round.

Let's say, for illustrative purposes, that you are making the smallest size sweater and you want to use the Big Star chart (see The Swatches: ESC Swatches), which is 17 stitches wide and 13 rows tall. You can easily add stripes or more rounds of the MC to make it tall enough. But how do you make this chart work for the stitch count?

First, divide the total number of stitches around the chest by the number of stitches in the chart that you want to use to find out how many times you can work the chart. 125 ÷ 17 = 7.35. This means that you can work the chart seven times and there are some leftover stitches. To find out how many stitches are leftover, first multiply the number of chart repeats by the number of stitches in the chart: 7 x 17 = 119 stitches. Then subtract this number from the total stitches around the chest: 125 - 119 = 6 stitches. So there are six stitches left over.

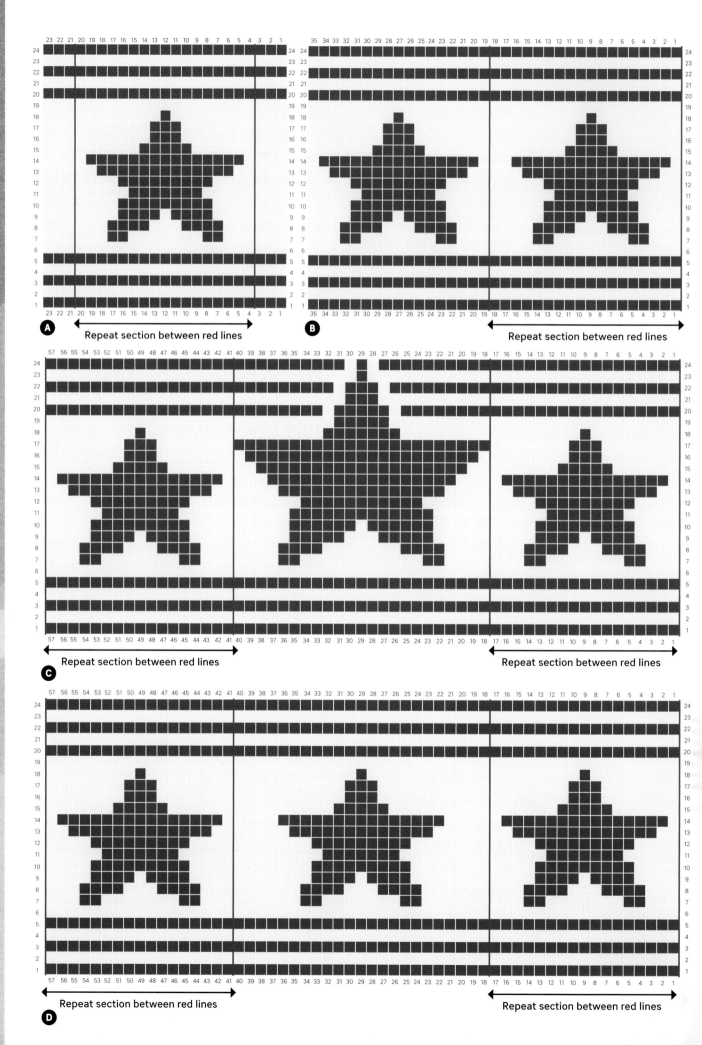

SWAPPING AND MODIFYING CHARTS

Next decide where the extra stitches should go. You could work three extra stitches at each end of the charted section **(A)**, distribute them between repeats of the chart (one stitch between each repeat) **(B)**, or you could add them to the center back. Because there are an odd number of repeats of the chart, there will be a star centered at the center back, so you would need to alter the star at the center back to accommodate the six extra stitches (making a wider star) **(C)** or place three extra stitches at each side of the center back star **(D)**.

The same principles can be applied to the Sleeve sections. Use the stitch count across the widest section of the sleeve colorwork for your calculations and then add the sleeve shaping back in later, referring to the sleeve chart for the size you are working on. For example, for the smallest size sweater, the stitch count across the colorwork section is 46. So 46 ÷ 17 = 2.7. This means two stars will fit across the sleeve with some stitches left over: 17 chart stitches x 2 repeats = 34 stitches. Subtract 34 stitches from the total number of stitches around the sleeve: 46 - 34 = 12 stitches. There are 12 stitches left over.

To distribute these extra 12 stitches you can use the same methods as on the body. The least complicated solution is to place them at the beginning and end of the chart. To visualize this, make a copy of the sleeve chart then cut it down the middle and insert the new chart in the center. We can distribute half (6) of the extra stitches to the right of the new chart repeats, and half (6) to the left **(E)**. Note that the 6 stitches are counted along the top edge of the sleeve; there are fewer stitches across the bottom of the chart, because of the sleeve shaping. Now we have a clear picture of the leftover stitches that are not part of the pattern repeat and we can fill them in with color however we like **(F)**. Note that I changed the non-stitches to gray so that the light-colored stitches in the chart would show up better.

Tip

Although it might seem time consuming, if you are making a more complicated chart swap it's best to make a complete new chart to be sure you like how it looks before you start stitching. There are free websites specifically for making these kinds of charts (I like to use stitchfiddle.com) but you can also use Excel, or plain ol' colored pencils and graph paper!

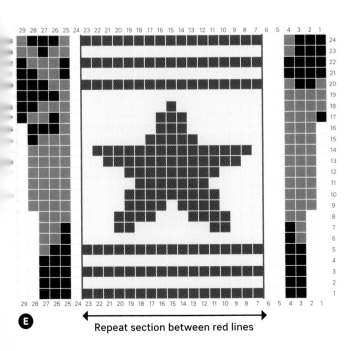

E   Repeat section between red lines

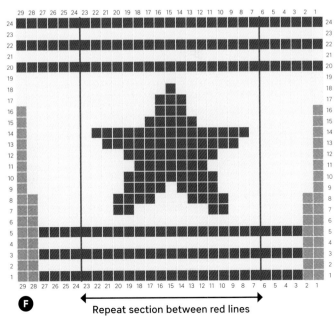

F   Repeat section between red lines

SNOWY PICTURE HAT

This project has lots of options for swapping. Look for a chart that has a 20 st repeat for a 1:1 swap. Or alternatively 60, 40, 30, 15, 10, 8, 5, 4, 3, 2 stitch repeats would work as well. There are 34 rounds before decreases start at the crown of the hat. You certainly do not need to bring the colorwork up that far if your chart isn't as tall. Dotty (see The Swatches: SESC Swatches), Forest, Howl, Istanbul, Leopard Print, Soft Serve (see The Swatches: ESC Swatches), Great Divide (see The Swatches: CSC Swatches), would all work well, just to name a few.

TREAD SCARF

This project was made to showcase any ESC colorwork pattern, just adjust the length of the scarf to fit. The number of stitches in the scarf = the number of pattern repeat stitches x number of repeats. Add 4 sts to this: 2 in MC at end where you fasten off, and 1 MC stitch at the beginning of each row plus 1 for the beginning chain.

For example: to use the Runs with Scissors chart (see The Swatches: ESC Swatches) which has a 32-stitch repeat, and repeat it 9 times, work the math as follows: 32 x 9 = 288 sts. To make the border on the scarf with the same color as the scissors, add two more stitches—one for each end in the background color—so the scissors don't blend into the edging. So now we have 288 + 2= 290. Then add two stitches for the end edging, and one for the beginning edging plus one chain for the turning chain on the Set-up Row: 290 + 2 + 1 + 1 = 294 sts for the foundation chain.

Note: We only have one stitch at the beginning for the edging but two at the ending because a beginning chain is made in this first stitch that doesn't count as a stitch—it adds a thickness to the beginning border to match the width of the two stitches at the end. And because the Scissors pattern ends with a solid row of background color, you will likely want to add one at the beginning of the scarf to balance out the colorwork.

For an easy, no-math swap-out substitution, choose a stitch pattern that has an 8-stitch repeat and work as many rows as necessary to get to the scarf width that you want. The following would work well: Open Weave, Scattered Diamonds, Vibrations, or Escher Cubes (see The Swatches: ESC Swatches).

CLADDAGH MITTENS

You will need a small chart of 20 sts and 14 rounds. Swap out rounds 5–19 of the Claddagh Upper Chart with Rounds 2-16 of Heart Breaker (see The Swatches: CSC Swatches) adding one column of MC to each end. Swap Rounds 6–19 of the Claddagh Upper Chart with Rounds 2-15 of Tiny Unicorn (see The Swatches: SCBLO Swatches) or Delftware (see The Swatches: FPDC Swatches). Or swap out Rounds 5–19 of the Claddagh Upper Chart for Rounds 1–15 of Bunny Love (see The Swatches: FPDC Swatches) omitting the hearts (just work those in the MC). Or center one repeat of Nellie the Elephant (see The Swatches: CSC Swatches) OR Narwhal School (see The Swatches: SESC Swatches) instead of the claddagh, filling in with MC as illustrated **(G and H)**.

ICICLES PULLOVER

Waves of Grain, Diamond Mountain, Girl's Best Friend (see The Swatches: ESC Swatches), Gardens, Phases (see The Swatches: CSC Swatches), and Amplified (see The Swatches: SCBLO Swatches) all have the same number of stitches and rows, and the visual center is in the same place. Easter Island (see The Swatches: SCBLO Swatches) has the same number of stitches, and if the bottom row of the chart counts as the set-up row, then it would have the same amount of rows, too. Choose whether or not to work the little diamond from the decrease chart. It will line up visually with the above list of charts, but if you decide not to use it, you can work in solid MC from that chart (in other words, do not use CC except to work over it when directed).

Cupcakes (see The Swatches: ESC Swatches), Lucky Horseshoe (see The Swatches: FPDC Swatches), and Village (see The Swatches: SCBLO Swatches) have the same number of stitches and have the visual center in the same place (stitch #7), however, there are fewer rounds in the chart. If you wanted to use any of these charts, you could make a pattern of simple stripes above and below the charted image until you get the right number of rounds, or you can add more rounds in just the MC (either above or below or some of both) to fill in the extra rounds of the chart **(I and J)**.

MODIFYING CHARTS FOR OTHER REASONS

If you are working on a colorwork chart, and you are unhappy with the clarity of your stitches, keep in mind that you can flip your chart so that you can work the mirror image of it. For example, if you want to work a chart from this book that has a strong right diagonal motif, and you want to work it in the ESC stitch pattern (which has jagged lines when on a right diagonal), you can flip the chart to work the mirror image. This will make your diagonal lines smoother as they will be left-sloping. Another thing to keep in mind is that you can rotate a chart 90 degrees and work it sideways. This technique can be helpful when working a sideways constructed scarf—your charted image does not need to be sideways on the scarf. Rotating the chart will require you to do a small swatch first, however, as it will affect the overall appearance of your colorwork.

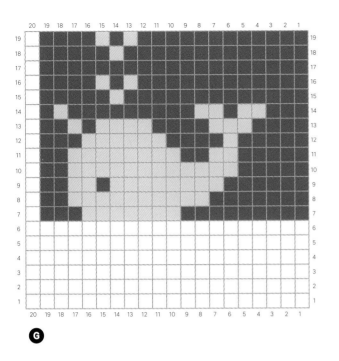

G

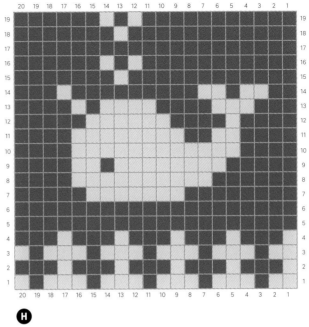

H

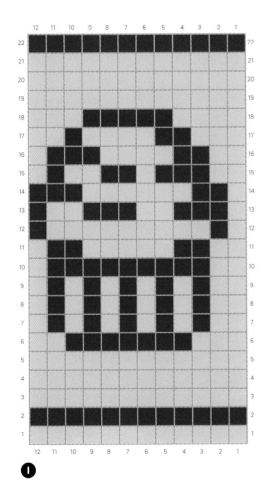

I

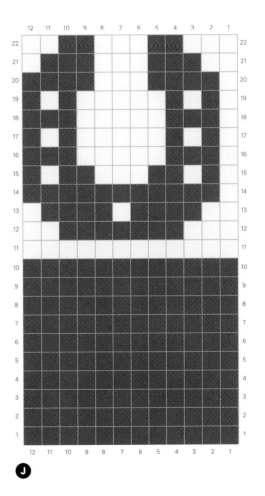

J

About the Author

Brenda K. B. Anderson crochets, knits, and sews into the wee hours after her kids have gone to bed. She loves designing stuffies that make her laugh, and accessories that beg to be worn over and over again by her friends and family. Brenda is the author of *Beastly Crochet* and *Crochet Ever After* and also teaches on Craftsy. She designs for numerous crochet publications and yarn companies and is managing editor of the *Creative Crochet Corner*. Brenda lives in a little house in Saint Paul, MN where it is sweater weather nine months of the year.

Shout-outs!

This book wasn't made by me—it was made by all of us! It first originated years ago and has been helped along by so many wonderful and talented people to become something truly special!.

First, I need to acknowledge the original Interweave team with an extra-heartfelt thanks to the amazing Kerry Bogert for planting the seed in the first place. Without her, this book would truly not exist. Then there was Daniella Nii's eagle-eye expertise, and Nathalie Mornu's very patient and kind encouragement.

And then came the incredible David and Charles crew: Ame Verso brought this book to life; she believed in it from the very beginning, understood what it should become and helped me to get it there. I am so grateful to Jessica Cropper, Jeni Chown, Sam Staddon, Jason Jenkins and of course the very patient Marie Clayton and Lindsay Kaubi for pooling their talents to turn my rambling thoughts and swatches into a user-friendly, informative and beautiful book!

And a super-special thank you to Molly Cacek, who has always encouraged me from the very beginning of my yarn-career. Molly swooped in with her crochet hook held high to help me finish up the swatches for this book. Without her crochet talents I would surely still be swatching.

Throughout the process of designing the charts, I relied very heavily on my sister Lisa and my husband Aaron to tell me if my designs "worked." I would text a chart (sometimes multiple times a day) and say "what is this?" Depending on their answer the charts were added to the collection or scrapped. Together they were the first filter; like a pre-editor to the entire project.

A big thank you to my both of my parents who taught me the value of making things myself. And to Anya and Ronnie—the best things I've ever had a hand in making.

Most of all, thank you to all of my fellow crocheters who have supported my work and encouraged and inspired me and my designs over the years. You are the reason I wrote this book!

Suppliers

And thank you so much to my suppliers for sending yarn support! Your yarns are always such an inspiration to me.

I can't wait to use them again. And a special thank you to **WeCrochet at Crochet.com**.

Berroco:
berroco.com

Brown Sheep Company, Inc:
brownsheep.com

Jameison's:
jamiesonsofshetland.co.uk

Malabrigo:
malabrigoyarn.com

O Wool:
o-wool.com

Index

A DAVID AND CHARLES BOOK
© David and Charles, Ltd 2023

David and Charles is an imprint of David and Charles, Ltd
Suite A, Tourism House, Pynes Hill, Exeter, EX2 5WS

Text and Designs © Brenda Anderson 2023
Layout and Photography © David and Charles, Ltd 2023

First published in the UK and USA in 2023

A catalogue record for this book is available from the British Library.

ISBN-13: 9781446309575 paperback
ISBN-13: 9781446382165 EPUB
ISBN-13: 9781446310458 PDF

This book has been printed on paper from approved suppliers and made from pulp from sustainable sources.

Printed in Turkey by Omur for:
David and Charles, Ltd
Suite A, Tourism House, Pynes Hill, Exeter, EX2 5WS

10 9 8 7 6 5 4 3 2 1

Publishing Director: Ame Verso
Managing Editor: Jeni Chown
Editor: Jessica Cropper
Technical Editors: Marie Clayton and Lindsay Kaubi
Head of Design: Anna Wade
Senior Designer: Sam Staddon
Design: Blanche Williams and Marieclare Mayne
Pre-press Designer: Ali Stark
Illustrations: Kuo Kang Chen
Art Direction: Laura Woussen
Photography: Jason Jenkins
Production Manager: Beverley Richardson

David and Charles publishes high-quality books on a wide range of subjects. For more information visit **www.davidandcharles.com**.

Share your makes with us on social media using **#dandcbooks** and follow us on Facebook and Instagram by searching for **@dandcbooks**.

Layout of the digital edition of this book may vary depending on reader hardware and display settings.

SWATCHES CROCHETED BY MOLLY CACEK

CSC Swatches
Bonbon
Phases
Carpeted
Gardens
Peaks and Valleys
Bosky
Secret Language of Yarn
Sideways Glances
Single Crochet!
Tiny Dancer
Writing on the Wall

FPDC Swatches
Bubbly
Cherries
Plait
Hand Sign
Skulduggery
Cross Winds
Maki
Puppy Love
Posy
Dinos
Spiders
Worlds Collide

SCBLO Swatches
Riptide
Buckled
Bolt from the Blue
Zigs and Zags
Helix
Tooth
Saguaro
Twin-tone Hearts
Umbrella
Village
Radiate